Be A Better Sales Leader

The Proven Systems to Unlock Greatness Within Your Team

Kristin Gutierrez

Praise for Be A Better Sales Leader

Kristin's authenticity, passion for the craft, and expertise based on 'real world' B2B sales experience are more than enough to keep you engaged. Her 'Outcomes-based Framework' and innovative ways of examining 'Productivity' are more than enough to ignite your top line.

- Allison McDougall respected B2B Sales Executive and Mentor in the global pharmaceutical and e-commerce industry

Kristin provides valuable insights and actionable takeaways that can be immediately implemented to drive transformation within organizations. Her passion for helping companies create a positive and productive work environment is evident in her engaging and informative workshops. I highly recommend Kristin to any company looking to create a meaningful and transformative impact within their organization.

- Krista Mashore, 5-time best-selling author and named Yahoo Finance's number 1 digital marketer to watch in 2021

Kristin is an amazing and enthusiastic leader. She is passionate about helping people around her grow and develop professionally. Kristin is always looking for ways to improve an organization and works hard to help others grow with her.

- Ana Trejo, Senior Communications Manager

Don't let the title fool you. "Be A Better Sales Leader" by Kristin Gutierrez is a must-read resource for EVERY leader. Kristin is a master at providing practical strategies and insights that are an easy-to-follow roadmap for creating high-performing and motivated sales forces and teams. If you're seeking to cultivate a culture of excellence and drive remarkable results, this book is a must-read transformative book!

- Bomi Anise, Founder Lead 2 Impact and Author of upcoming book "The Brilliance Paradigm: Why Unlocking and Owning Our Brilliance Transforms the Way We Live and Lead"

Having witnessed Kristin's journey firsthand, I couldn't be prouder as her father. Her book, 'Be A Better Sales Leader,' reflects her deep understanding of the sales landscape and her unwavering commitment to helping organizations succeed. Through her workshops, she not only reengages employees but also taps into their inner brilliance, a true testament to her exceptional leadership skills. As a fellow Sales Manager who has helped several companies triple their sales and profits, I highly recommend this book for its valuable insights and actionable strategies that will elevate your sales team to new heights of success.

- Brent Hansen, Executive Sales Leader

Kristin is an amazing professional and motivation to women leaders across multiple industries. She comes with a fierce passion that overflows to make others want to work towards their goals, no matter how big or small. She is relatable and approachable, and I am always excited to see what she does next to help leaders reach their fullest potential!

– Sarah Coburn, Career Coach

I am absolutely delighted to endorse Kristin Gutierrez as an expert on sales. Her commitment to elevating the game and closing deals is incredible. Her unwavering leadership qualities combined with her razor-sharp sales techniques, undoubtedly forms an unbeatable culture of excellence that produces exceptional results. Kristin's unique talent to lay down a clear vision, instill accountability, all while operating from a place of authenticity places her in a class of her own. If maximizing their potential is the goal, any sales team would be lucky to have her on board.

- Anitha Panicker, CEO & Founder of Growth GOAT, Leadership Speaker, and Coach.

Dedication

To my sons Gibson and Jack,

This book is dedicated to both of you, my shining stars. From the moment you entered my life, you have brought immense joy and love into every day. You are my inspiration, my motivation, and my constant reminder of the importance of growth and personal development.

Gibson, my energetic and curious 4-year-old, your zest for life and thirst for knowledge amaze me every day. Your enthusiasm is contagious, and your determination to explore and understand the world around you is truly inspiring. Never stop asking questions, my little explorer, and remember that there is no limit to what you can achieve.

Jack, my sweet and playful 2-year-old, your infectious giggles and love of sports light up my heart. Your gentle spirit and loving nature remind me of the power of empathy and connection. As you continue to grow, always remember the importance of kindness and compassion in everything you do.

Both of you hold a special place in my heart, and I dedicate this book to you as a reminder of the endless possibilities that await you in life. May it serve as a guide to help you become the best versions of yourselves, both personally and professionally. Always follow your dreams, believe in your abilities, and never be afraid to chase your passions.

Thank you for being my greatest teacher and for filling my life with boundless love and joy. I am forever grateful to be your parent and to witness your incredible journeys unfold.

Foreword by Belinda Hilbert

In the first few months of 2021, I was facing major burnout – after a year of COVID lockdowns and the emotional strain that came with it, I simply couldn't bring myself to get focused or find the drive in my career the way I had for the ten years before. I was proud of my decade of experience in operational management and was comfortable with the respect and perspective that brought. But work that I used to enjoy suddenly felt overwhelming, or worse, pointless – and I didn't know how or what to do to get out of my funk.

And that's when fate handed me a giant energizer battery who was fully charged: Kristin entered my professional life right when I needed a push, and without me even realizing it was happening I forged a new, stronger direction forward and fell back in love with that thing we all do 40 hours a week - work. Collaborating first as colleagues, her zest was contagious and it wasn't long before I approached her with a wild idea: Could I change my core professional role from operations to sales? And could I join her team? And by could, I didn't mean should – I meant would.

Would I fall flat on my face because I had no idea how to sell?

I didn't fall flat onto anything. Instead, I grew so much in the year after I was onboarded to Kristin's team that I didn't recognize the burned-out, exhausted person I had been. I learned that it's not what you do, but the why of you doing it that is the true source of fire – and by tapping into that passion, I was able to take all my experience and perspective with me on a whole new career path.

In the pages that follow, I know you'll be able to find your own path – by focusing on what lights you, you'll refocus on your leadership with renewed drive, energy & focus. By investing your time in this book, you are taking a chance – just like I took in my own career. I know you won't regret it.

So, let this book be your guide, your energizer, and your source of inspiration. Embrace the journey, and may it lead you to a place of fulfillment and success beyond your wildest dreams.

Table of Contents

Chapter 1
Why We're Here

Round Peg Square Hole

Did you ever experience unclear expectations from senior leadership or need to learn how to communicate with the executive team in your organization?

Or you're a mid-level manager who wants to improve your leadership skills and drive success for your team but needs a guide to get you from this role to the next.

Did you ever feel like you were in a role that needed a clear path to do the job?

Maybe you knew you were made for the job but felt like an imposter living your dream?

Are you looking to become a better sales leader and take your team to new heights? To be seen as a visionary and innovator within your role? To cross-functionally manage and continue to climb the corporate ladder?

Did you receive adequate training on the tools, processes, and strategies you need to succeed in your role? Or have you been faking it til you make it hoping you figure it out before someone notices?

Several challenges face leaders:

1. **Lack of Experience:** New sales leaders may need to gain experience managing a sales team, setting targets, and developing strategies to achieve those targets.
2. **Unclear Expectations:** New sales leaders may need clear expectations set by their organization, which can lead to confusion and uncertainty about their role.

3. **Communication Issues**: Sales leaders may need help communicating effectively with their team members, leading to misunderstandings and misalignment of goals and priorities.
4. **Resistance to Change:** Sales leaders may encounter resistance from team members who resist change, making implementing new processes or strategies challenging.
5. **Inadequate Training:** New sales leaders may need adequate training on the tools, processes, and strategies they need to succeed.
6. **Lack of Resources:** Sales leaders may need access to the resources and support they need to build and manage a successful sales team.
7. **Pressure to Perform:** New sales leaders may feel pressure to perform right away, which can lead to stress and burnout.
8. **Difficulty Building Rapport:** New sales leaders may need help to build strong relationships with their team members and clients, which can lead to low morale and poor performance.
9. **Inconsistent Sales Processes: Sales** leaders may face challenges in establishing and implementing consistent sales processes across the team, leading to inefficiencies and missed opportunities.
10. **Time Management:** Sales leaders may have a lot on their plate, including managing the team, attending meetings, reviewing reports, and handling administrative tasks. This can make it difficult to prioritize tasks and manage time effectively.
11. **Limited Budget**: Sales leaders may have limited budgets and resources, making investing in the tools and resources needed to drive success difficult.
12. **Lack of Support:** Sales leaders may feel isolated and unsupported in their role, leading to frustration and burnout. With adequate support and mentorship, new sales leaders may navigate the challenges of their roles and achieve success.

Sounds daunting. But there is a better way.

By providing the right resources and support, organizations can set their sales leaders up for success and ensure they can achieve their goals.

New sales leaders need support, guidance, and training to overcome these challenges and succeed.

Most leaders face challenges and obstacles during their careers. One of the hardest things leaders may have to overcome is managing difficult team members or situations. This could include dealing with employees who could perform better, resolving conflicts among team members, or navigating complex organizational politics.

I have been leading since I was a kid – bossing around my siblings during our "on-screen" debuts with our 1990 camcorders. Ask my dad for the home movies. I was a retail store leader throughout college. And I have been a corporate leader since 2005, at 24.

It is possible to lead from a place of confidence, even without an instruction book, and there are three effective ways to unlock greatness within yourself and your team.

This book is about sales leadership and everything getting better as a leader.

You can immediately apply the learning from this book to your everyday leading life. The three pillars are easy to follow and implement. You can pick and choose which section will pertain to you and your team(s), or you can read the book cover to cover.

Leaders often look to up-level their skills and implement strategies that successful sales leaders use to drive revenue and motivate their teams. I know that's what I am looking for!

This book is my unique perspective on becoming a better sales leader based on the theory and application of real-life experience and the research of others who are subject matter experts in this space.

I love to help clients get immediate transformational results in a workshop designed to help your capable teams combat burnout, stay engaged, find self-fulfillment, boost creativity, drive innovation, and improve social selling.

The key to driving transformation and overcoming challenges is to develop strong leadership skills, build a strong support network, and remain open to learning and growth.

Leaders who can navigate these obstacles with grace and resilience are often the ones able to achieve the most tremendous success and make the most significant impact.

I didn't want to write this book. I had to. Because I didn't have an instruction manual for any of my roles. I always had earned my stripes as an individual contributor, and when promoted, I was thrown into the mix and expected to level up.

I'm comfortable failing forward, but I know many who aren't.

I had to learn failure is feedback. That when you fall, you get right back up. I had to become willing to assume more risk – and I was looking for books and mentors to help me go from A to Z but couldn't find exactly what I needed, so I needed to write this book.

Hoping that if it helps at least one other person, then it would have been worth it.

If I wrote this book and helped just one person be a better sales leader, it would all be worth it!

As you work through these chapters, please join the conversation online and let me know how I can best support you.

#beabettersalesleader

Cheering you on,

Kristin

Chapter 2
Promoted Without An Instruction Book

Fake It 'Til You Make It

In 2005 a year after graduating college, I worked as an Inside Sales Rep (ISR) at 22 years old for the first time in Corporate America.

The job was in the translation and localization industry, which I knew nothing about, working for a UK-based publicly traded company called SDL International (now known as RWS) as their first experimental inside sales representative.

I soaked up everything I could about this job in an industry completely foreign to me.

I lived in downtown Chicago in 2005. And I'll never forget the sheer joy I felt riding the bus home with my boss, Elise Thompson, and asking her many questions about our industry, client requirements, understanding the industry verbiage. It was so fun! I soaked up everything I could find, including the industry magazine, Multilingual.

What happened over the coming three years was magic. I was mentored and trained by THE BEST of the best in the localization industry!!

One person was Allison McDougall, who, over the years, went from mentor to boss to friend.

As an ISR, I quickly learned the ins and outs of the industry. I was responsible for prospecting new customers, qualifying leads, and setting up appointments for the outside sales team. Allison rolled up her sleeves and taught me strategy, mapping of accounts, persistence, empathy, and the importance of logging activity in our offline version of Goldmine CRM!

Within a year of working at SDL, I was promoted to Manager of Global Inside Sales. This was a trip because I was now leading a small team of Inside Sales reps, mainly in the UK.

Flying blind took on a whole new meaning for me.

I'll never forget the pride I felt when the promotion came in, followed by utter fear and embarrassment. Would my new team know I was "faking it 'til I made it"?

How would I quickly learn what was expected of me? And how would I adapt to all these new responsibilities? Who would I ask for help when I had a problem? Would my peers treat me differently? Would I be met with resistance or skepticism? This can lead to feelings of anxiety, stress, and self-doubt.

Not only that, but this promotion meant I had a new boss. Whereas my boss as an ISR was Elise, who sat down the hall for me, now my boss was in the UK headquarters! Clive Thomas would become my second corporate boss ever, and I later realized his actions would help instill in me leading from a place of confidence.

Over the next two and a half years, several times a year, I was flying overseas to train my team – all much older than me. I was only 24! My parents were always like, You do what?! For whom!? LOL.

When we acquired another massive company in our space (Idiom), I led their team of Inside Sales reps. I was responsible for managing my growing team of ISRs, overseeing the sales process, and driving revenue growth.

Want to know the kicker?

I didn't know what I was doing. I didn't have an instruction manual. I wish I had known how much you needed to innovate within your role.

No one taught me how to manage up.

No one taught me how to manage a team.

No one taught me the little things I needed to do every day, no matter what, to drive productivity.

No one taught me how to grow within my role and continue to climb the ladder.

One foot in front of the other, I started to figure it out. I learned what was expected of me. I learned how to communicate effectively. How to deal with uncertainty.

And you know what?

I was good at it! I would write sales processes and best practices for leading my inside sales team. I met face to face with the CEO of a then $300M company on the value add of my team to the organization.

Being promoted into a leadership role can be exciting and daunting, especially when you feel you need all the skills and knowledge needed to excel in your new position.

It's natural to feel overwhelmed and even a little intimidated, but it's important to remember that being a leader is not about knowing everything. It's about having the right mindset and attitude and being willing to learn and grow.

Like Dara Khosrowshahi, CEO of Uber, said in a March 2023 interview, "You have to have the heart to stick it out as a leader."

If you find yourself in this position, here are some tips that may help you navigate your new role:

Embrace the challenge: Instead of feeling intimidated by your new position, embrace the challenge. Remember that your employer saw something in you that made them believe you could handle this role, so trust in yourself and your abilities.

Be open to learning: No one knows everything, especially regarding leadership. Be open to learning from others, including your team members, peers, and superiors. Ask questions, seek feedback, and don't be afraid to admit when you don't know something.

Build relationships: As a leader, building strong relationships with your team members is essential. Take the time to get to know each individual, their strengths and weaknesses, and what motivates them. This will help you build trust and create a positive work environment.

Focus on your strengths: While being aware of your weaknesses and working on improving them is essential, remember to focus on your strengths. Identify what you bring to the table and how you can use your strengths to benefit your team and organization.

Don't be afraid to make mistakes: Leadership is a learning process, and everyone makes mistakes. Don't be afraid to make mistakes but be willing to learn and improve. It's better to try and fail than to not try at all.

Being promoted into a leadership role when you don't feel fully equipped can be challenging, but it's also an opportunity to learn and grow. Embrace the challenge, be open to learning, build relationships, focus on your strengths, and don't fear making mistakes. You can excel in your new role and become a successful leader with the right mindset and attitude.

I needed to figure that out on my own, and that's why I'm writing this book. I hope that at least one person will benefit from these lessons learned and the action plan I now use so you, too, can succeed.

And I didn't give up!

I learned to fail forward, ask for help and seek mentors.

Now with almost 20 years of experience, I'm putting everything I learned and then some into this book.

The purpose of this book is for my lessons learned to help others be better leaders. Can't wait for you to dive in!

Chapter 3
Overcoming Imposter Syndrome

Borrowed Confidence

I was talking to someone recently who was getting into yoga for the first time and how they were doing yoga at home to "get it right" before going into the studio. *You can imagine the advice they were receiving on heading into the studio to make sure their form was correct to help avoid injury, the community aspect of yoga, and how it's a judgment-free zone, but I digress.*

But you can relate if you've ever been to a yoga class. I know I can! And the imposter is real.

I'm not perfect. What will everyone else think of my poses? I don't know how to do chaturanga. What if I need a break? Why is no one else drinking water? I need water!! LOL

The reality is I've never overcome imposter syndrome more than at yoga. From 14 to 34 weeks pregnant, I took on a 20-week yoga teacher training. Practicing 200 hours of yoga while learning to teach (even when not pregnant) is no joke. Hot yoga. Vinyasa yoga. Yin yoga. Hot yoga. Snoring in class yoga….

It is humbling when you're used to being super competitive, and now you spend the entire class in child's pose because you have pregnancy-induced carpal tunnel in both wrists.

Suddenly, it doesn't matter what anyone thinks.

Because what is getting me through is knowing I'm working toward a bigger goal.

And then it happens.

Somewhere in there, your mission kicks into overdrive. You become confident in your choices. Why you're there. What your goals are. Why they're important.

At first, you fake it a little until you make it. But you keep going. You find confidence in your choices. And you realize no one else is thinking about you.

All they are thinking is, can THEY hold Warrior 3 during the hold. They aren't thinking about you.

This confidence helps you overcome the imposter.

Let me say that (safely) practicing hot yoga at 39 weeks pregnant brings out your inner warrior and busts through imposter syndrome.

Hold on to that next time the imposter comes at you.

The same can be true for leadership.

I suffer from imposter syndrome every single day.

And I'm not exaggerating.

The amount of pressure from all over is exhausting.

Do I have what it takes to talk on that stage? What will the person bigger than me, better than me, smarter than me, think of me?

Is everyone judging me for writing this book? What will this person or that person think of me? What if no one buys it? What if they think I need to be better at discussing this subject?

The list goes on.

Recognizing it is often the first step on the path to overcoming it. Because once you realize you're facing an imposter, you can reframe your thinking to help yourself overcome it.

Here's what Amy Porterfield has to say on the subject:

"I've been talking a lot about courage this past week. I've had to really tap into this myself.

Being confident doesn't mean you're never afraid or doubt yourself. It means you acknowledge those feelings but don't let them hold you back. It means being brave enough to take that first step, even if it feels uncomfortable. And let me tell you, I've had to remind myself of this more times than I can count. But every time I've pushed through my fears and doubts, I've come out stronger and more confident on the other side.

So if you're feeling scared or unsure, know that you're never alone. It's okay to feel those things. But don't let them stop you from pursuing your dreams and living the life you want. Keep pushing forward and trust that you have what it takes to succeed.

Overcoming imposter syndrome can be a challenging process, but it is possible with some effort and the right mindset. Allow me to break down a few strategies that can help you overcome imposter syndrome and achieve your goals with confidence.

From the article "Beating Impostor Syndrome at Work" by Proactive IT Recruitment, it is quoted, "Remember, nobody is perfect. It's natural to want to strive for perfection, but it's important to acknowledge that mistakes will happen. If you make a mistake, own it, learn from it, and move on. Don't let the fear of failure hold you back. Accept that you will experience setbacks and challenges, but also recognize that you have the skills and abilities to overcome them. By focusing on your strengths and achievements, you can build confidence and overcome the feelings of self-doubt that come with impostor syndrome."

Acknowledge your accomplishments

One of the first steps to overcoming imposter syndrome is to acknowledge your accomplishments. It's easy to focus on your failures and shortcomings, but it is essential to remember that you have achieved many things in your life. Reflect on your successes and the challenges you have overcome. Write them down and celebrate them.

Recognize that everyone experiences self-doubt.

It is essential to recognize that everyone experiences self-doubt in their lives, and imposter syndrome is a familiar feeling among high achievers. Many successful people have talked openly about their struggles with imposter syndrome, including Maya Angelou, Albert Einstein, and Michelle Obama. Recognizing that you are not alone in feeling this way can be a powerful reminder that imposter syndrome is a normal part of the human experience.

Challenge your negative self-talk.

Negative self-talk is a common symptom of imposter syndrome. It's easy to fall into a cycle of self-criticism and self-doubt, but it is important to challenge these negative thoughts. When you notice yourself engaging in negative self-talk, try to reframe your thoughts in a more positive light. For example, if you think, "I don't deserve this promotion," try reframing it to, "I worked hard for this promotion and deserve to be recognized for my accomplishments."

Learn to accept constructive feedback.

Many people with imposter syndrome have a difficult time accepting constructive feedback. They may see it as a sign of failure or evidence they are not good enough. However, constructive feedback can be an opportunity to learn and grow. Instead of seeing it as a negative, try to reframe it as a positive opportunity to improve.

Surround yourself with supportive people.

Having a supportive network of people around you can be helpful in overcoming imposter syndrome. Surround yourself with people who believe in you and your abilities. Seek mentors or coaches who can provide guidance and support. Join groups or organizations that align with your interests or goals. Having a solid support system can help you feel more confident in your abilities and less alone in your struggles.

Set realistic goals

Setting realistic goals can help you build confidence and overcome imposter syndrome. Instead of setting unrealistic expectations for yourself, break your goals down into smaller, achievable steps. Celebrate your progress along the way and focus on the positive aspects of your accomplishments.

Practice self-care

Self-care is an essential aspect of overcoming imposter syndrome. Taking care of your physical and mental health can help you feel more confident and grounded. Make time for activities that bring you joy and relaxation, such as exercise, meditation, or spending time with loved ones. Prioritizing self-care can help you feel more balanced and less overwhelmed by the pressures of work or other responsibilities.

Keep learning and growing.

Finally, it is crucial to keep learning and growing to overcome imposter syndrome. Seek opportunities to expand your knowledge and skills, whether through continuing education, training programs, or other professional development opportunities. The more you learn.

Embrace your failures

Many people with imposter syndrome have a fear of failure. They may believe that any mistake or misstep is evidence of their inadequacy. However, failure is a natural part of the learning process. Embrace your failures as opportunities to learn and grow. Recognize that every successful person has experienced failure in their life. Reframe failure as a necessary step on the path to success.

Take action despite your fears.

Fear is a common barrier to overcoming imposter syndrome. People with imposter syndrome may hesitate to act because they are afraid of failing or being exposed to fraud. However, it is crucial to take action despite your fears. Recognize that your fears are usual, but don't let them hold you back from pursuing your goals. Take small steps towards your goals, even if they feel scary or uncertain. Each step forward will help build your confidence and reduce your feelings of imposter syndrome.

Practice self-compassion

Self-compassion is a powerful tool for overcoming imposter syndrome. Treat yourself with the same kindness and understanding you would offer to a friend who is struggling. Recognize that imposter syndrome is a familiar feeling and that you are not alone in your struggles. Practice self-care and self-compassion by giving yourself permission to rest, reflect, and recharge.

Keep a success journal.

Keeping a success journal can be a helpful tool for overcoming imposter syndrome. Please write down your accomplishments, no matter how small they may seem. Celebrate your successes and reflect on the hard work and effort that went into achieving them. Keeping a success journal can help you focus on the positive aspects of your life and build confidence in your abilities.

Reframe your thoughts

Reframing your thoughts can be a powerful tool for overcoming imposter syndrome. Instead of thinking in terms of success or failure, try reframing your thoughts in terms of growth and learning. Instead of thinking, "I failed at this task," try reframing it to, "I learned a valuable lesson from this experience." Reframing your thoughts can help you see challenges as opportunities for growth and reduce feelings of inadequacy.

Seek professional help

If your feelings of imposter syndrome are interfering with your daily life or causing significant distress, it may help to seek professional help. A therapist or counselor can help you work through your self-doubt and develop strategies for building confidence and self-esteem.

Practice gratitude

Practicing gratitude is a powerful way to overcome imposter syndrome. Take some time each day to reflect on the things you are grateful for in your life. Focus on the positive aspects of your life and the things that bring you joy and fulfillment. Practicing gratitude can help shift your focus away from self-doubt and towards the positive aspects of your life.

Set boundaries

Setting boundaries is an important aspect of overcoming imposter syndrome. People with imposter syndrome may take on too much to avoid disappointing others or to prove their worth. However, overextending yourself can lead to burnout and increased feelings of self-doubt. Learn to say no to requests that are beyond your capacity or don't align with your goals. Set clear boundaries around your time and energy, and prioritize activities that bring you joy and fulfillment.

Overcoming imposter syndrome is a journey that requires recognizing it's there and implementing these strategies to overcome it.

Confidence is another strategy for overcoming imposter syndrome. And it deserves a section all its own.

If imposter syndrome is a feeling of self-doubt and inadequacy that can prevent individuals from recognizing their own achievements and abilities, then confidence is a critical factor in overcoming imposter syndrome.

People with imposter syndrome often struggle to feel confident in their abilities and may fear being exposed as frauds. However, building confidence can help individuals overcome imposter syndrome and achieve their goals.

Confidence is vital for several reasons. First, confidence helps individuals believe in themselves and their abilities. People with imposter syndrome often struggle to believe they can achieve their goals. They may doubt their abilities and fear they will fail. However, confidence can help individuals recognize their strengths and abilities. When individuals are confident in themselves and their abilities, they are more likely to take risks and pursue their goals.

Second, confidence helps individuals deal with failure and setbacks. People with imposter syndrome often fear failure, as they may see it as evidence of their inadequacy. However, failure is a natural part of the learning process. Individuals are better equipped to deal with failure and setbacks when they are confident in themselves and their abilities. They are more likely to bounce back from failure and try again rather than give up.

Third, confidence helps individuals communicate effectively. People with imposter syndrome may struggle to communicate their ideas and thoughts effectively. They may fear that their ideas will be rejected or that they will be exposed as frauds. However, confidence can help individuals communicate their ideas with clarity and conviction. Individuals are more likely to speak up and share their ideas when they are confident in themselves and their abilities.

Building confidence is essential in overcoming imposter syndrome.

Confidence helps individuals believe in themselves and their abilities, deal with failure and setbacks, and communicate effectively.

By recognizing their strengths and achievements, challenging negative self-talk, acting despite their fears, practicing self-care and self-compassion, and seeking support from others, leaders can build their confidence and overcome imposter syndrome.

With time, effort, and perseverance, you can recognize you are worth it, have the potential, and achieve your goals with confidence and resilience and overcome imposter syndrome.

Worksheet: Overcoming Imposter Syndrome

Acknowledging your achievements and strengths can boost your confidence and remind you of your value. By answering these questions, sales leaders can gain meaningful outcomes, such as improved confidence, a greater sense of self-worth, and the ability to tackle new challenges with resilience and self-assurance.

What are your accomplishments and strengths

You can improve your self-confidence and self-esteem by recognizing negative self-talk and replacing it with positive affirmations.

How can you challenge negative self-talk?

Seeking support from mentors, colleagues, or a professional coach can provide valuable feedback and guidance and help you build your confidence.

Who can support you?

By embracing new challenges and learning opportunities, you can build your skills and feel more confident.

What opportunities for learning and growth does this new role present?

Taking care of your physical and mental health and practicing self-compassion can help you feel more grounded and confident.

How can you practice self-care and self-compassion?

Setting realistic goals and celebrating your progress along the way can build your confidence and momentum.

What are your realistic goals?

Being open to constructive feedback can help you grow and develop your skills and abilities and feel more confident in your role.

How can you learn from feedback?

Recognizing that imposter syndrome is common among high achievers can help you feel less alone and more confident in yourself.

How can you remember that self-doubt is normal?

Chapter 4
Success Leaves Clues

Always Ask One More Question

Many sales leaders strive for greatness but don't know where to start. I know I didn't. The three pillars of becoming a better sales leader were born from that.

When I analyze where I am today and how I got here, I compare myself to other leaders I respect and admire.

My husband makes fun of the number of online courses I've purchased in the last 10 years. I get it. But I have these innate tendencies to mirror others and follow their success.

You need not spend what I've spent to succeed. You just had to pick up this book and implement the strategies I'm sharing for free.

A few respected leaders in my inner circle have to say about it:

Michele Smith, CEO of MoPop says, "One of the biggest things, especially going through the pandemic, was working on emotional intelligence and just really working on the empathy of working with your employees through crises in leadership. And I think that's a big area of focus for a lot of C-suite or any organization with their employees that are leading. And so for me getting to this path has been really working with mentors that are my colleagues and friends or other women that I've really admired in the industry and not just in business development talking about leadership and just trying to hone my style."

Stefan Huyghe, Vice President Sales, says, "I discovered that there's no single best way to learn how to be a great leader. I believe the best way to learn how to be a great leader is to be open to learning and growth and to actively seek out opportunities to develop your skills and knowledge. I try to practice regular self-reflection and I contemplate my success as I have failures on a daily basis as much as my personal values and belief systems. Over the years, I've become much more self-aware, and I would like to think that today I make much more intentional leadership decisions than in the past."

Remember, when the going gets tough... Just keep going!

My team inspires me DAILY in their drive to keep their foot on the gas despite all the twists, turns, and bumps in the road.

Success leaves clues and one of the most effective ways to learn and grow as a leader is to observe and mirror the behaviors and skills of those who have excelled in the role. When you study successful leaders, you can gain valuable insights into what it takes to achieve great results and develop the skills and competencies needed to succeed.

One of the main reasons success leaves clues when being a leader is that successful leaders have a track record of achievement. They have achieved significant results, overcome obstacles, and demonstrated the ability to lead and inspire others. By studying successful leaders, you can learn from their experience and apply their strategies to your leadership approach.

Another reason success leaves clues is that successful leaders have a set of skills and competencies tested and refined. These skills and competencies include communication, strategic thinking, problem-solving, emotional intelligence, and building and maintaining relationships. By observing successful leaders and mirroring their behaviors and skills, you can develop these competencies and become a more effective leader.

Successful leaders often have a clear and compelling vision for the future. They can communicate this vision in a way that inspires and motivates others to work towards a common goal. You can learn how to develop and communicate your vision for your team or organization by observing successful leaders.

Another way success leaves clues is through the relationships that successful leaders have built. Successful leaders often have strong relationships with their team members, stakeholders, and other industry leaders or community leaders. You can develop stronger relationships with the people in your professional network by observing successful leaders and mirroring their relationship-building skills.

One of the best ways to observe successful leaders and learn from their experience is through mentorship. A mentor has succeeded in their career and will share their knowledge and experience with others. By seeking a successful mentor, you can learn from their experience, gain valuable insights into the leadership role, and develop your own leadership skills.

In addition to mentorship, you can also learn from successful leaders through reading books, attending conferences and seminars, and networking with other professionals in your industry or community. By exposing yourself to different perspectives and approaches to leadership, you can develop a well-rounded understanding of what it takes to be a successful leader.

Remember, success leaves clues when being a leader. By observing and mirroring the behaviors and skills of successful leaders, you can develop the competencies needed to achieve great results, build strong relationships, and inspire and motivate others. Seek mentorship, read books, attend conferences and seminars, and network with other professionals to learn from the experience of successful leaders and develop your leadership skills.

Check out these other books about sales and sales leadership:

1. *Sales Management Simplified* by Mike Weinberg is a book that provides practical advice on how to lead and manage sales teams effectively. The author draws on his experience as a sales consultant and trainer to offer insights into the fundamentals of sales success and how to build a high-performing sales team.

The book comprises four key components: leadership, talent management, sales culture, and sales management activities. Weinberg emphasizes the importance of setting clear expectations, holding salespeople accountable, and focusing on the fundamentals of sales success, such as prospecting, qualifying, and closing deals. He also offers insights into building a sales culture that supports and motivates salespeople to achieve their goals and developing effective sales management activities that drive results.

Throughout the book, Weinberg provides numerous examples and case studies to illustrate these principles in action. He offers valuable insights and strategies for anyone looking to improve their sales management skills, regardless of their industry or job title. By focusing on the basics of sales success and providing practical advice on building a high-performing sales team, "Sales Management Simplified" offers a straightforward and accessible approach to sales management that can help companies achieve sustainable growth and success.

2. *Cracking the Sales Management Code* by Jason Jordan is a book that offers a data-driven approach to sales management. The author draws on his experience as a sales consultant and trainer to provide practical advice for how to identify and measure key performance indicators (KPIs) that relate to your organization's specific sales goals.

The book comprises three key components: strategy, process, and people. Jordan emphasizes the importance of developing a sales management strategy aligned with your organization's goals and values. He guides how to identify the KPIs most relevant to your sales process. He also offers insights into optimizing the sales process, from lead generation to customer acquisition, and building a high-performing sales team by hiring and training the right people.

Throughout the book, Jordan provides numerous examples and case studies to illustrate these principles in action. He offers valuable insights and strategies for anyone looking to improve their sales management skills, regardless of their industry or job title. By focusing on the data and analytics that underpin successful sales organizations, "Cracking the Sales Management Code" offers a fresh and innovative approach to sales management that can help companies achieve long-term success.

3. *The Sales Acceleration Formula* by Mark Roberge is a book that provides a data-driven approach to building and scaling a successful sales organization. The author draws on his experience as a senior executive at HubSpot, a leading marketing and sales software company, to offer practical advice on leveraging technology and analytics to improve sales performance.

The book is organized around Roberge's Sales Acceleration Formula based on four key components: hiring, training, process, and technology.

Roberge emphasizes the importance of hiring coachable, analytical, and methodical salespeople, and he provides guidance on developing effective training programs that align with these qualities. He also offers insights into optimizing the sales process, from lead generation to customer acquisition, and leveraging technology to improve efficiency and effectiveness.

Throughout the book, Roberge provides numerous examples and case studies to illustrate these principles in action. He offers valuable insights and strategies for anyone looking to improve their sales performance, whether a startup or an established enterprise. Focusing on the data and analytics that underpin successful sales organizations, "The Sales Acceleration Formula" offers a fresh and innovative approach to sales that can help companies achieve long-term success.

4. *SPIN Selling* by Neil Rackham is a research-based approach to sales that emphasizes the importance of asking questions to identify a customer's specific needs and pain points. The book is based on a comprehensive study of thousands of sales calls, and it offers practical advice on how to sell effectively by focusing on the customer's perspective.

The SPIN selling approach is based on four types of questions: Situation questions, Problem questions, Implication questions, and Need-payoff questions. By asking these questions in a structured way, salespeople can uncover their customer's needs and concerns and offer solutions that meet those needs. The book provides numerous examples and case studies to illustrate these principles in action. It offers valuable insights and strategies for anyone looking to improve their sales performance, regardless of their industry or job title.

5. *The Challenger Sale* by Brent Adamson and Matthew Dixon challenges the traditional view of sales. It suggests that the most successful salespeople challenge their customers' assumptions and offer unique insights to help them improve their businesses. The book is based on extensive research and interviews with thousands of salespeople and customers, and it offers practical advice for how to succeed in today's rapidly changing business environment.

Adamson and Dixon argue that the most effective salespeople are "challengers" who take a different approach than traditional "relationship builders" or "hard workers." Challengers are defined by their ability to teach, tailor, and take control of the sales process, and they are highly skilled at identifying and addressing their customers' needs and concerns. By focusing on these core competencies, challengers can build customer trust and credibility and ultimately achieve greater sales success. The book offers numerous examples and case studies to illustrate these principles in action, and it provides valuable insights and strategies for anyone looking to improve their sales performance.

6.   In his book "To Sell is Human," Daniel Pink argues that selling is no longer the sole domain of traditional salespeople but a skill that is increasingly necessary in almost every profession. Pink suggests that the ability to persuade others is essential in today's world, where people are bombarded with information and have more choices than ever before. He offers practical advice for how to sell effectively, emphasizing the importance of empathy, attunement, buoyancy, clarity, and purpose.

Pink's book challenges traditional assumptions about sales and offers a more nuanced and complex view of what it means to sell. He suggests that effective selling requires not just the ability to make a sale but also the ability to build long-term relationships with customers, to identify their needs and concerns, and to offer solutions that meet those needs. By recognizing the importance of selling in a broader context, Pink's book offers valuable insights and strategies for anyone looking to improve their sales skills, regardless of their industry or job title.

7.   In his book "The 7 Habits of Highly Effective People," Stephen Covey outlines seven habits he believes can help individuals achieve personal and professional success. The first three habits focus on personal effectiveness: being proactive, beginning with the end in mind, and putting first things first. Being proactive means taking responsibility for one's own life and choices, while beginning with the end in mind involves visualizing and working towards long-term goals. Putting first things first means prioritizing tasks based on their importance and urgency.

The next three habits focus on interpersonal effectiveness: thinking win-win, seeking to understand, then to be understood, and synergizing.

Thinking win-win involves seeking mutually beneficial outcomes in all interactions while seeking first to understand involves listening to others and trying to see things from their perspective before sharing your own. Synergizing means working collaboratively with others to achieve shared goals while respecting and valuing their contributions. Covey argues that by developing these seven habits, individuals can become highly effective in all aspects of their lives, from their relationships to their careers.

Chapter 5
3 Pillars to Becoming a Better Sales Leader

Trust Fall

In 2022, I lost $30,000 trying to build out an Amazon store deactivated by Amazon less than 6 months later.

In 2018 I chose a job that felt like career suicide.

I've been passed up for promotions and new roles more times than I can count throughout my career.

In 2014, I got divorced less than a year into my marriage.

In the past 6 years, I started and stopped 6 businesses.

The point?

You'll probably fail 10X more than you'll ever succeed.

And that's GOOD! Because learning to fail forward builds in you all the traits you'll need when you finally succeed

When you do win, because you will, that win feels that much better knowing how hard you worked for it.

Keep going!

What I realized from personal experience, talking with other great leaders, and doing research are the consistent themes around what being a great leader means, and I knew I had to write this book to share these pillars with you!

Here are 3 PILLARS you need to do to become a better sales leader:

1.   **Get out of your own way**. How do you get out of your own way? You fail forward, ask for help, and seek a mentor or two. You demonstrate your willingness to grow into your role and improve your mindset.

2.   **Daily habits and the compound effect.** Can you create a system of processes specific to your team – such as sales rigor –executed because of a deep-rooted culture within the team and allows you to evolve the processes over time and report to the Executive team on progress, risks, and gaps? This is a winning combination. Rolling out processes. Having said processes, be adapted within your team. Uses the metrics and outcomes from the processes to manage your manage and report on KPIs.

3.   **Professional development**. What is your professional learning plan? Are you engaged on LinkedIn and creating a multi-faceted brand that represents you, your strengths, your team, your company, your industry, and your interests?

Becoming a better sales leader requires action and commitment to continuous growth. I've never seen another book on the market that addresses these areas for improvement, and that's why I'm so excited to teach you how to use these pillars to unlock greatness within your team!

Worksheet: Be A Better Sales Leader Worksheet

Becoming a better sales leader requires action and commitment to continuous growth. This worksheet will guide you through the steps to get ahead and elevate your leadership and sales skills.

Step 1: Get out of your own way

- Identify any limiting beliefs, biases, or habits that may hinder your success as a sales leader.
- Write them down and reflect on how they have affected your performance.
- Develop a growth mindset by reframing negative self-talk and embracing a culture of learning and experimentation.

Step 2: Daily habits

To become a better sales leader, it's important to implement daily habits that foster success. Here are three daily habits to help you excel in your role:

- Rigor in the Sales Process
- Create a structured sales process that provides a clear path for your team to follow.
- Monitor progress and identify areas for improvement in your team's performance.
- Regularly review and refine your sales process to optimize results.
- Culture and Empathy
- Foster a positive sales culture that encourages collaboration and innovation.
- Practice empathy and actively listen to your team to understand their needs and concerns.
- Celebrate wins and acknowledge hard work to boost morale and motivation.
- Managing Up
- Build a strong relationship with your manager by understanding their goals and priorities.

- Proactively communicate with your manager to inform them of your team's progress and challenges.
- Seek opportunities to align your team's goals with your manager's goals to demonstrate your value to the organization.

By implementing these daily habits, you can enhance your leadership skills, foster a positive team culture, and achieve greater success in your role as a sales leader. Remember, consistency is key - commit to practicing these habits every day to see results.

Step 3: Continue to grow personally and professionally

- Attend conferences and networking events to stay up to date with industry trends and best practices.
- Read books and articles related to sales leadership and personal development.
- Seek mentorship or invest in ongoing training and development opportunities.

By acting on these steps, you can be on your way to becoming a better sales leader. Use this worksheet as a guide to help you stay on track and achieve greater success and fulfillment in your career.

Remember, continuous growth and learning are essential to success, so keep pushing yourself to be the best you can be.

Chapter 6
Get Out of Your Own Way

How to Eat an Elephant

Progress and building confidence are key to getting out of your own way.

I am not in the business of empowering you to meet your quota. I teach you confidence and your confidence will come from the progress of skills, and your confidence will come from the assurance that you know what to do and which steps to take to crush it.

That is why I do what I do so you say, "I have the confidence to crash my quota," "I have the confidence to lead a team," or "I have the confidence to step into a new role and be successful doing it."

If there's one thing I've learned since 2005, managing others is that you'll never have all the answers. You need to learn from others – both those within your company who you admire and are doing your job or a similar job well and those who are outside your company, maybe even outside your industry, but who you admire because they are great leaders.

As a sales leader, it's essential to be aware of any roadblocks or limitations that may hinder your team's success.

And while time is of the essence, go easy on yourself. How do you eat an elephant? One bite at a time!

I want this to be a valuable resource for anyone new to managing people or wanting to advance from their role today into a bigger one. To get out of your own way, consider these strategies:

Develop self-awareness: Self-awareness is crucial for identifying and addressing any personal biases, blind spots, or limiting beliefs that may affect your leadership style. Consider taking personality assessments, receiving feedback from others, or working with a coach or mentor to improve your self-awareness.

Delegate effectively: It's important to trust and empower your team members to take on responsibilities and make decisions. Delegating effectively can free up your time and allow you to focus on higher-level tasks, such as strategy development or building relationships with key clients.

Listen actively: Listening to your team members' perspectives, concerns, and feedback can help you identify areas where you may be unintentionally obstructing their success. Listening to their needs and ideas can also help you build trust and foster a more collaborative team environment.

Encourage experimentation: Innovation and experimentation can lead to new ideas and solutions to drive sales success. Encourage your team members to try new approaches and strategies, and provide them with the resources and support they need to experiment and learn.

Embrace a growth mindset: A growth mindset involves viewing challenges and failures as opportunities for learning and growth. By adopting this mindset, you can model a positive, solution-focused attitude that inspires and motivates your team members to overcome obstacles and achieve their goals.

I've told so many stories throughout this book to provide examples to help you learn from the experiences of others and gain insights into how to handle different management situations.

Build foundational knowledge

Another strategy for getting out of your own way is to build foundational knowledge in key areas such as **communication, delegation, motivation**, and **performance management**. This knowledge can provide a solid framework for your management approach.

Develop new skills

Always be learning. Invest in yourself and your team. Managing people is an ongoing learning process. Even if you are experienced in management, there are areas where you can improve your skills. Reading management books, attending workshops, and hiring trainers can help you stay current with the latest trends and best practices in leading, which can help you be a more effective manager. For example, you may learn about different coaching, mentoring, or conflict-resolution approaches.

Gain confidence

Managing people can be daunting, especially if you are new to it. Check back in Chapter _ on overcoming imposter syndrome and how confidence can help you soar in your career.

Refresh your perspective

Even if you have been managing for a long time, staying open to new ideas and perspectives is important. Reading management books can help you refresh your perspective on management and provide you with new ideas and strategies to try.

Learn about emerging trends.

The business world is constantly evolving, and new trends and best practices in management are always emerging. Reading management books can help you stay current with the latest trends and techniques, which can help you be a more effective manager.

Refine your approach

No manager is perfect, and there is always room for improvement. Reading management books helps you identify areas where you can refine your approach and become an even better manager.

Learn from others' experiences.

Even experienced managers can benefit from learning from the experiences of others. A management book can provide insights into how other successful managers have approached common management challenges.

While you may have a lot of experience managing salespeople, get out of your way to help refresh your perspective, learn about emerging trends, develop new skills, refine your approach, and learn from others' experiences. You can become an even more effective leader by staying open to new ideas and continuing to learn.

Improving Mindset and Leading with Confidence

Mindset is everything. Ask Thomas the Train. No really. Thomas the Train can teach sales leaders several valuable lessons about mindset and confidence. Here are some of those lessons:

Thomas's confidence in his abilities is unwavering, even when faced with obstacles. As a sales leader, you must have self-belief and confidence in yourself and your team's capabilities, especially when tackling difficult sales targets or obstacles. A positive and confident attitude can inspire your team and help you overcome challenges more effectively.

Thomas is always eager to try new things and explore new territories, even if it means leaving his comfort zone. As a sales leader, it's important to be open to change and innovation and encourage your team to do the same. Embracing change can help you stay ahead of the competition and adapt to new market trends and customer needs.

Thomas makes mistakes but always learns from them and uses them to improve. As a sales leader, it's essential to recognize that mistakes are a natural part of the sales process, and you should encourage your team to learn from them. Treating mistakes as opportunities for growth and learning can help your team develop resilience and a growth mindset.

Finally, Thomas is part of a larger team of trains that work together to achieve their goals. As a sales leader, it's crucial to foster a sense of teamwork and collaboration among your team members. Encouraging open communication, sharing ideas, and supporting each other can help your team work more effectively toward a common goal.

How do you overcome a bad mindset?

As a student of Dean Graziosi's in 2010, I learned a lot about conquering mindset.

Dean Graziosi is a well-known entrepreneur and motivational speaker who has written several books on personal development and mindset. Here is a quote from him on the importance of mindset:

"Your mindset is everything. It's what you think and feels that drives every action you take in life. It's the lens through which you see the world and the filter that determines what you focus on. If you want to achieve your goals and live your

dreams, you need to cultivate a mindset of positivity, growth, and abundance. You need to believe in yourself, take action toward your goals, and embrace failure as an opportunity to learn and grow. Your mindset is the foundation of your success, and it's up to you to shape it into something powerful and empowering."

So what do mindset and confidence have to do with becoming a better sales leader?

Think about when you had your favorite outfit on, felt great about your hair, and wore your best smile. How did it make you feel? Confidence is a feeling. It's a way you carry yourself. Confidence is contagious.

You can overcome challenges with a better mindset, and confidence in your leadership abilities will be transferred to your direct reports and Executives.

Here are three hacks to help you get out of your own way, fail forward, take full accountability, and grow beyond your leadership role:

1.   **Practice self-awareness**: It's important to be aware of limiting beliefs and self-doubt. One way to do this is through journaling or regular reflection time. Write down negative thoughts or beliefs holding you back and challenge them with evidence to the contrary. This can help you shift your mindset and get out of your own way.

2.   **Seek feedback**: Ask for feedback from your team, colleagues, and mentors. This can be uncomfortable, but it's important to hear both positive and negative feedback to improve. Listen carefully to what others have to say and take it as an opportunity for growth and learning.

3.   **Embrace failure**: Failure is a natural part of the learning process, and embracing it as an opportunity for growth is important. Rather than viewing failure as a reflection of your abilities, see it as a chance to learn and improve. Take full accountability for your actions and learn from your mistakes so you can do better next time.

By practicing self-awareness, seeking feedback, and embracing failure, you can get out of your own way and grow beyond your leadership role. These hacks can help you take full accountability for your new role and become a more effective leader.

Worksheet: Improving Mindset

Identify your current mindset: Take a few minutes to reflect on your current mindset. Are you generally optimistic and positive, or do you focus on negatives and obstacles? Write down a few words or phrases that describe your current mindset.

Recognize limiting beliefs: Consider any beliefs about yourself or the world that may hold you back. For example, do you believe that you're not good enough, that success is only for other people, or that you'll never be able to achieve your goals? Write down any limiting beliefs that come to mind.

Challenge your limiting beliefs: Take each of your limiting beliefs and ask yourself if they're really true. Is there any evidence that contradicts these beliefs? What would happen if you believed the opposite? Write down any new, more empowering beliefs you come up with.

Practice gratitude: Gratitude is a powerful way to shift your mindset from one of lack to one of abundance. Take a few minutes each day to write down three things you're grateful for. These can be big or small things but try to focus on the positive aspects of your life.

Set goals: Setting goals can help you focus your energy and motivate you to take action. Write down three short-term goals (goals you can achieve within the next few weeks or months) and three long-term goals (goals you'd like to achieve within the next year or more).

Take action: Finally, take action towards your goals. Break them down into smaller, manageable steps and work towards them consistently. Celebrate your successes along the way and use any setbacks as opportunities to learn and grow.

Remember, improving your mindset takes time and effort, but you can develop a more positive, empowered outlook on life with practice.

Chapter 7
Fail Forward

Dress For The Job You Want, Not For The Job You Have

Failing forward is a concept that has gained increasing recognition in recent years as a mindset and strategy for personal and professional growth. It is a way of viewing failure not as an endpoint or a reason to give up but as a valuable learning experience that propels us to success. This idea pertains to the experience of becoming a better leader, where the challenges and expectations can be high, and mistakes are almost inevitable.

As a sales leader, feeling overwhelmed and unsure of oneself is easy. Whether coming into a new organization or taking on a new role within the same company, there will likely be new responsibilities, new people to manage, and new goals to achieve. This can be a lot to take on, and it is natural to feel some anxiety and self-doubt.

Say, for example, you're stepping into a new role in your current company and will now manage your former peers.

Managing former peers can be a challenging experience for many new managers. Here are strategies that can help to overcome the fear of managing colleagues who used to be peers:

The dynamic has changed: As a new manager, it's important to recognize that the dynamic between you and your former peers has shifted. While you may have been friends or colleagues before, your role now involves managing and directing their work. Acknowledge this change and be clear about your expectations.

Establish clear boundaries: One way to address this new dynamic is to establish clear boundaries between your personal and professional relationships. While it's still possible to be friends with your former peers, you need to separate your personal feelings from your professional responsibilities.

Communicate effectively: Effective communication is key when managing former peers. You must provide clear direction, constructive feedback, and hold your team members accountable for their work. This requires open and honest communication, as well as active listening skills.

The key to overcoming these challenges is to adopt a mindset of failing forward. This means recognizing that setbacks and failures are essential to the learning process and using them as opportunities to grow and improve. **Instead of seeing failure as a reason to give up or feel discouraged, it is an invitation to reflect, learn, and adapt.**

One of the most important aspects of failing forward as a new manager is to be open and honest about one's mistakes. This can be challenging, especially when one is still building relationships and establishing oneself in a new role. However, being transparent and taking responsibility for one's errors is essential for building trust with one's team and demonstrating a willingness to learn and improve.

In addition, leaders should be proactive in seeking feedback from their team members and colleagues. This can be an invaluable insight into areas where one can improve and where one is doing well. Feedback is not a criticism but an opportunity to learn and grow, and a new manager receptive to feedback will be better positioned to succeed in the long term.

Another key aspect of failing forward as a leader is to develop resilience and persistence in the face of setbacks. Inevitably, there will be obstacles and challenges along the way, but a manager who can maintain a positive attitude and stay focused on the bigger picture will be more likely to succeed eventually. This means not giving up in the face of adversity but instead using setbacks as opportunities to learn and grow.

Finally, sales leaders need to embrace a growth mindset. This means seeing challenges and failures as opportunities for growth rather than fixed limitations. A growth mindset recognizes that talent and intelligence are not fixed traits but can be developed through hard work and persistence. By adopting this mindset, new managers can approach their role with optimism and a willingness to learn and adapt.

Failing forward is an essential mindset and strategy for new managers to adopt as they navigate the challenges of their role. By recognizing that setbacks and failures are opportunities for growth and learning, being open and transparent about one's mistakes, seeking feedback, developing resilience and persistence, and embracing a growth mindset, new managers can position themselves for long-term success. While the road may be bumpy, those who approach their role with a spirit of curiosity and a willingness to learn will ultimately achieve the greatest success.

"Dress for the job you want, not the job you have" is an adage that emphasizes the importance of projecting a professional image in the workplace. How we dress and present ourselves can significantly impact how others perceive us and can even influence our behavior and mindset.

All too common now is the CEO wearing t-shirts and blue jeans, and with office culture different than what it was pre-pandemic, we won't focus on the physical aspect of dressing for the job you want. Know that your professional appearance affects how you perceive your own confidence and how others perceive you.

Let's dive into using the adage dress for the job you want, not for the job you have, as an example of how to over-perform in your current role to be noticed as a capable candidate for a promotion or step-up roles at other organizations.

Imagine you're VP of Sales, and you have your sights set on the C-level.

The C-level, or the highest level of executive leadership in an organization, is a coveted position for many professionals. However, reaching this level requires strategic planning, hard work, and skill development. As a Vice President with your sights set on the C-suite, there are several key steps you can take to increase your chances of success.

Build strong relationships: One of the most important aspects of leadership is the ability to build and maintain strong relationships with colleagues, stakeholders, and customers. I tell my team this all the time.

Your internal "customers" are equally important (if not more sometimes) than your external customers.

Depending on how long you've been at your company or in your role, you likely have a network of contacts and relationships you can leverage to advance your career. However, continue cultivating these relationships and expanding your network, both within and outside of your organization. This can be done through networking events, industry conferences, and other opportunities to connect with peers and leaders in your field.

Develop a strategic vision: C-level executives are responsible for setting the strategic vision and direction of the organization. You can start developing your strategic thinking skills by looking beyond your current role and department and considering the broader goals and objectives of the organization. You can also seek opportunities to lead cross-functional initiatives or projects that require a more holistic view of the organization.

Build a diverse skill set: C-level executives need to lead across multiple functional areas, from finance and operations to marketing and human resources. As a Vice President, you can start developing your skills in these areas by seeking opportunities to lead projects or initiatives outside of your immediate area of expertise. Consider pursuing professional development opportunities, such as executive education programs or certifications, to expand your skill set.

Develop your leadership style: The most effective leaders have a clear leadership style aligned with their values and personality. As a Vice President, you can start developing your leadership style by reflecting on your strengths and weaknesses as a leader, seeking feedback from colleagues and mentors, and studying the leadership styles of successful executives. You can also seek opportunities to mentor and coach others, which can help you develop your leadership skills while also contributing to the development of others.

Demonstrate your value: To be considered for a C-level position, you must demonstrate your value to the organization. This can be done by consistently delivering results, building strong relationships, and contributing to the organization's overall success. You can also seek opportunities to lead high-profile initiatives or projects with a significant impact on the organization. By demonstrating your value in these ways, you can position yourself as a valuable asset to the organization and increase your chances of being considered for a C-level position.

Seek mentors and sponsors: Mentors and sponsors can be critical in advancing your career and helping you reach the C-level. A mentor can provide guidance and advice on career development, while a sponsor can advocate for you and help you gain visibility within the organization. As a Vice President, you can seek mentors and sponsors within your organization or industry, or you can consider joining professional organizations or networking groups that can provide access to potential mentors and sponsors.

Reaching the C-level as a Vice President requires strategic planning, hard work, and skill development. By building strong relationships, developing a strategic vision, building a diverse skill set, developing your leadership style, demonstrating your value, and seeking mentors and sponsors, you can position yourself for success and increase your chances of reaching the highest levels of executive leadership.

Remember, reaching the C-level is about more than what you do in your current role but also about how you position yourself for future opportunities and continue to develop your skills and leadership abilities.

Chapter 8
Ask For Help: Seek Mentors

Don't Reinvent the Wheel

It's 2005.

After plastering my resume all over the internet, I ended up at SDL (RWS Group) as their first Inside Sales rep.

What happened over the coming 3 years was magic.

I was mentored and trained by THE BEST of the best!!

One of those people was Allison McDougall.

She rolled up her sleeves and taught me strategy, mapping of accounts, persistence, empathy, and the importance of logging activity in our offline version of Goldmine CRM! LOL

And over the years, she went from mentor to boss to friend.

If Allison were the only mentor I had in my career, I would be so fortunate because she really did impact me from then to now.

But it's not a coincidence I've sought mentors throughout my career and am grateful for them all.

One time, about 12 years into my career, I left my salaried job to take a contract job at NetApp to work inside the Globalization Program Strategy Office, mainly to put myself near smart strategic senior leaders all respected in their roles. It paid off 100X over. The career move was brilliant!

And, when I needed a full-time salary again because I had my first kid, I leveraged the experience and maintained the relationships.

My current CEO is a mentor. I joined this company because of him when he was VP of Global Operations 3 years before becoming CEO.

The list goes on.

Finding a mentor can be valuable to gain insights and guidance from someone with more experience and knowledge than you. Here are tips on finding a mentor:

Identify your goals and needs: Before you start looking for a mentor, take some time to think about your goals and needs. What do you hope to gain from a mentorship relationship? What areas of your personal or professional life would you like to improve? Clearly understanding what you are looking for can help you find a mentor who is a good fit.

Look for someone who shares your values and interests: When looking for a mentor, it's important to find someone who shares your values and interests. This ensures that you have a good working relationship and are committed to the same goals.

Network and ask for recommendations: Networking is a great way to meet potential mentors. Attend industry events, join professional organizations, and connect with others on social media platforms like LinkedIn. You can also ask colleagues, friends, or family members for recommendations.

Be proactive and reach out: Once you have identified potential mentors, be proactive and contact them. Explain your goals and interests and ask if they would meet with you to discuss mentorship opportunities. Be respectful of their time and expertise and be willing to work around their schedule.

Be open and receptive: When working with mentors, be open and receptive to their feedback and guidance. Be willing to learn, grow, and seek their advice and insights.

Overall, finding a mentor can be a valuable way to gain insights and guidance from someone with more experience and knowledge than you. By identifying your goals and needs, networking and asking for recommendations, being proactive, and being open and receptive, you can find a mentor to help you achieve your goals and reach your full potential.

Chapter 9
Daily Habits

The Compound Effect

3 Meaningful Actions Great Sales Leaders Take Every Day

Do you ever experience unclear expectations from senior leadership or need to know what's expected of you from the executive team in your organization?

Or you're a mid-level manager who wants to improve your leadership skills and drive success for your team but lack a guide to get you from this role to the next.

Are you looking to become a better sales leader and take your team to new heights? To be seen as a visionary and innovator within your role? To cross-functionally manage and continue to climb the corporate ladder?

As a sales leader, it's essential to inspire and guide your team to success while driving business outcomes. How do you become a more effective leader?

To increase the net outcomes of your sales team, increase leads, add more deals, win more revenue, and crush your team quota, be consistent with your actions and output.

Here are three meaningful daily actions that great sales leaders take to make an impact.

1.   Check-in with your teams: It might sound obvious, but how often do we get sucked into the daily grind and forget to pause and check in? Checking in with your team can be subdivided into three main buckets: individual people's needs, the microculture of the team, and cross-functional business needs. Let's take a quick look at each:

a.   People: It is ALL about your people. It has to be. And every day, great leaders remember this with a people-first approach. Are you asking every team member how they are? Are you asking questions about their families? What things do they have going on outside of work? Are you empathizing? Are you compassionate? This is above and beyond your 1-2-1's, team meetings, etc.

    b.   Culture: Is your team culture still "in-check" for the day/week/month/quarter? Is the team living out the culture code the team created at the beginning of the year? Is the team chat running if the one who keeps it going is out of the office? (And I hope this isn't the leader). Does everyone feel genuinely connected? Are they asking questions and getting answers?

    c.   Cross-functional business needs: Are there any intradepartmental dependencies being ignored? Have you checked in with your peers? Is collaboration continuing with key departments peripheral to your team? You and your team should communicate clearly with the other departments in your organization so deadlines stay on track. One day you will really need something from them, so lead from a place of proactivity.

    2.   Follow up on deals/tasks/revenue/quota: Another key area of focus every great sales leader acts on daily is numbers! Sales leaders often ask, what are the key metrics I should be measuring? While every organization is different, here is a baseline:

    a.   Dashboards/KPIs: Do you have team-specific dashboards in your CRM to measure items that are both important to the business and important to you? The business might already track activity on a centralized dashboard. Great, clone it into yours. But what about a quarterly contest you want to run in your team. Track those metrics in your team dashboard, too! Other metrics to measure include deal amounts and accuracy of deal probability, revenue to quota, tasks on anything with revenue potential, and so much more! Make it a conscious effort to review the reports and dashboard views weekly with your team, whether in a 1-2-1 or team meeting.

    b.   Which deals are "stuck": Another way to put this is who needs help? Or what can we do to push a deal over the line? Sometimes, it's coordinating a brainstorming session with a broader team to make sure the strategy is on point. Other times it's leveraging an executive to call in a favor or email to help advance a deal.

    c.   Managing up: My favorite hack. First ask yourself, is your boss approachable or intimidating? Are they open to opinions, or is it their way or the highway? Do they prefer to get down to business, or do they ask you questions about things outside of work? How do they consume information: via email, PowerPoint, Excel, or talking through the details? Knowing their persona will help you have more meaningful interactions with them. And regarding your boss, meaningful means measuring your effectiveness as a sales leader and whether you're doing your job.

3. Innovate: As a salesperson and leader, driving innovation is critical. There are several ways to use innovation to add value to you as a leader. You can demonstrate an innovative approach to a client's problem by repackaging a current solution to drive value or using innovation internally to drive continuous improvement in your organization. That's where my brain fires on all cylinders, and the fun starts because innovating requires interacting with globally dispersed teams and rolling up our sleeves both on the ground floor and strategically with stakeholders. Driving innovation is so much easier when you create a team within a team that is all bought in on the plan. Innovation and continuous improvement

To increase the net outcome of your sales team, increase leads, add more deals, win more revenue, and crush your quota, the compound effect of these three daily meaningful actions will help to make you a great sales leader.

A leader would want to uplevel their skills for several reasons, including:

To improve their ability to lead: By up leveling their skills, a leader can become more effective in leading their team and achieving organizational goals.

To stay relevant: The world is constantly changing, and leaders need to stay up to date with the latest trends and best practices in their industry. Upleveling their skills can help leaders stay relevant and avoid becoming obsolete.

To inspire their team: When leaders uplevel their skills, they set an example for their team members and inspire them to do the same. This can create a culture of continuous learning and development within the organization.

To increase their value: When leaders have broader skills, they become more valuable to their organization. This can lead to increased job security, higher salaries, and greater opportunities for advancement.

To enhance their personal growth: Learning new skills can be fulfilling, and help leaders feel more confident and capable in their role. This can lead to increased job satisfaction and overall happiness.

Overall, up-leveling skill is a key strategy for leaders who want to stay competitive, effective, and relevant in their role and for those who want to support the growth and development of their team.

1. Set clear goals and priorities for themselves and their team.
2. Communicate effectively with their team members and stakeholders.
3. Listen actively and with empathy to the concerns of their team members.
4. Build and maintain positive relationships with their team members.
5. Foster a culture of trust and transparency within the team.
6. Encourage creativity and innovation among team members.
7. Provide constructive feedback and recognition to team members.
8. Stay informed about industry trends and developments.
9. Take calculated risks and make informed decisions.
10. Continuously learn and develop new skills.
11. Delegate tasks effectively and empower team members to take ownership.
12. Stay organized and manage their time effectively.
13. Lead by example and demonstrate the behaviors they expect from their team members.
14. Build diverse and inclusive teams that value different perspectives.
15. Foster a sense of community and shared purpose within the team.
16. Remain adaptable and flexible in the face of changing circumstances.
17. Stay focused on the bigger picture while attending to details.
18. Build and maintain a positive mindset and attitude.
19. Manage conflicts and difficult situations with grace and respect.
20. Inspire and motivate team members to achieve their best work.

What is the big career goal you're working toward this year? And what is the number one thing holding you back from accomplishing your goal? Is there something in this free guide you could use more information on, such as driving innovation, managing up, or measuring KPIs?

The compound effect can have a profound impact on leading teams. At its core, the compound effect is the idea that small actions or decisions, taken consistently over time, can add up to significant results. Small changes, repeated consistently, can create a positive or negative effect that grows over time.

When applied to leading teams, the compound effect can be a powerful tool for success. Leaders who understand the compound effect can create a culture of continuous improvement and build momentum toward achieving their goals. However, leaders who fail to appreciate the power of the compound effect may find that small mistakes or missteps can snowball into larger problems.

One way that the compound effect can affect team leadership is through the concept of habit formation. Habits are the small actions or behaviors we repeat consistently. By consistently practicing positive habits, teams can build momentum toward achieving their goals. For example, a leader who consistently encourages open communication within their team can create a culture of transparency and trust. Over time, this culture can lead to better collaboration, increased creativity, and improved performance.

But negative habits can also have a compound effect. For example, a leader who consistently fails to address poor performance or behavior within their team can create a culture of complacency and low expectations. Over time, this culture can lead to decreased productivity and morale.

Another way that the compound effect can affect team leadership is through the concept of incremental progress. Leaders who understand the compound effect recognize that progress is rarely made in large, dramatic leaps. Instead, progress is typically made through small, incremental steps. By breaking down larger goals into smaller, achievable milestones, teams can create a sense of momentum and build confidence in their ability to succeed.

However, leaders must remember that the compound effect can work in positive and negative directions. If a team consistently fails to meet its goals or misses deadlines, this can create a negative cycle that can be difficult to break. Leaders must be proactive in addressing these issues and taking corrective action before they become ingrained in the team's culture.

The compound effect can also affect team leadership through the concept of feedback loops. Feedback loops are the mechanisms by which small changes can be amplified. For example, a leader who consistently provides constructive feedback to their team can create a culture of continuous improvement. Over time, this feedback loop can lead to better performance and higher levels of engagement.

Conversely, a leader who consistently provides negative or unhelpful feedback can create a culture of defensiveness and mistrust. Over time, this feedback loop can lead to decreased morale and decreased productivity.

Finally, the compound effect can affect team leadership through the concept of momentum. When a team is making progress toward its goals, it can build momentum that can carry them through difficult times. Conversely, when a team is stuck in a rut or failing to make progress, this can create a negative momentum that can be difficult to break.

Leaders who understand the compound effect can use this knowledge to create positive team momentum. By consistently setting achievable goals and celebrating small wins, leaders can create a sense of momentum that can propel their team toward success.

The compound effect is a powerful concept that can profoundly impact leading teams. Leaders who understand the compound effect can create a culture of continuous improvement, build momentum toward achieving their goals, and avoid negative feedback loops. However, leaders who fail to appreciate the power of the compound effect may find that small mistakes or missteps can snowball into larger problems. By applying the principles of the compound effect to team leadership, leaders can set their teams up for success and achieve their goals more effectively.

Worksheet: Consistency of Efforts Over Time in Leading Teams

The following worksheet helps you reflect on the concept of consistency of efforts over time and how it applies to leading teams. Answer the questions below to better understand how you can use consistency of efforts to build momentum and achieve success as a team leader.

1. What is the consistency of efforts over time? a. How can consistency of efforts be defined in leading teams? b. Why is it important for team leaders to understand the consistency of efforts over time?

2. How does habit formation relate to the consistency of efforts over time? a. What positive habits can a team leader encourage within their team? b. What are negative habits that a team leader should avoid?

3. How can incremental progress contribute to the consistency of efforts over time? a. How can a team leader break down larger goals into smaller, achievable milestones? b. What are strategies that a team leader can use to create a sense of momentum through incremental progress?

4. What is the role of feedback loops in the consistency of efforts over time? a. How can a team leader use feedback loops to create a culture of continuous improvement? b. What are some negative feedback loops that a team leader should know and avoid?

5. How does momentum relate to the consistency of efforts over time? a. How can a team leader build positive momentum within their team? b. How can a team leader break negative momentum and avoid getting stuck in a rut?

6. How can you apply the principles of consistency of efforts over time to your leadership style? a. What are specific actions that you can take to create a culture of continuous improvement and build momentum within your team? b. How can you hold yourself accountable for taking consistent actions over time to achieve your goals?

Reflecting on the concept of consistency of efforts over time and how it applies to leading teams can help you become a more effective leader. By understanding the power of small, consistent actions over time, you can create a culture of continuous improvement, build momentum toward achieving your goals, and avoid negative feedback loops. Use the insights gained from this worksheet to take actionable steps toward leading your team to success.

Chapter 10
Empowering Your Teams

Demotivation of Micromanaging

My first job out of college I was working at Saks Fifth Avenue on Michigan Avenue in Downtown Chicago.

The store has hundreds of employees. 3 months in a row I opened the most amount of Saks retail credit cards of all employees. I was #1 three months in a row.

I was an A+ worker. The person on the floor who cleaned up the most after my customers and my colleagues. The person who least stood around and gossiped with the others. Yet, there would be a shirt on the ground, and he would say "pick up that shirt" instead of picking up the shirt and asking if I can do it next time.

My boss, Israel, was a micromanager and it made coming to work unbearable. Had he met each team member where our individual strengths were, he would have seen more team cohesiveness, a cleaner store floor, increased sales, and more employee retention!

Empowering teams is a crucial aspect of successful organizations.

Empowerment involves giving team members the freedom to make decisions and take actions that align with the organization's goals and objectives.

It is an approach that encourages collaboration, fosters creativity and innovation, and promotes individual and team growth.

I wanted to first explore the concept of empowering teams and its benefits, as well as provide tips on how to empower your team effectively. And then, we will dive into the opposite of empowering teams: micromanagement.

<u>What is team empowerment?</u>

Team empowerment gives team members the autonomy and resources they need to make decisions, take ownership of their work, and contribute to the organization's success. It involves delegating authority and responsibility to team members, providing them with the information and tools, and encouraging them to take risks and experiment.

<u>The benefits of empowering teams</u>

Empowering teams has numerous benefits for the organization and its team members. Here are some of the most significant benefits of empowering teams:

Improved decision-making: When team members are empowered, they can make decisions faster and more effectively. They have access to all the information they need to make informed decisions, and a rigid hierarchy or bureaucracy does not constrain them.

Increased innovation and creativity: Empowering teams encourages innovation and creativity. When team members feel free to experiment and take risks, they are more likely to develop new ideas and solutions to problems.

Increased job satisfaction: Empowering teams gives team members a sense of ownership and control over their work. They are more likely to feel invested in their work and motivated to succeed.

Higher levels of engagement: Empowering teams leads to higher engagement among team members. They are more likely to be committed to the organization's goals and objectives and feel their contributions are valued.

Increased productivity: Empowering teams leads to increased productivity. When team members feel empowered, they are more likely to be motivated to do their best work and to take ownership of their tasks and responsibilities.

<u>How to empower teams</u>

Now that we've discussed the benefits of empowering teams, let's explore strategies for effectively empowering your team:

Set clear goals and expectations: Clearly defining goals and expectations is essential for empowering teams. When team members know what they are working towards, they can make decisions that align with those goals and objectives.

Delegate authority and responsibility: Delegating authority and responsibility is key to empowering teams. Team members should have the authority to make decisions and take actions that align with the organization's goals and objectives.

Provide resources and support: Empowering teams requires providing team members with the resources and support they need to succeed. This could include access to training and development opportunities and the tools and equipment.

Foster a culture of collaboration: A culture of collaboration is essential for empowering teams. Encouraging team members to work together, share ideas, and support one another creates a sense of community and helps to foster creativity and innovation.

Encourage risk-taking and experimentation: Encouraging team members to take risks and experiment is crucial for empowering teams. When team members feel free to try new things, they are more likely to develop innovative solutions to problems.

Provide feedback and recognition: Providing feedback and recognition is essential for empowering teams. Team members must know that their contributions are valued and that their efforts are making a difference.

Empowering teams is an essential aspect of successful organizations. It encourages collaboration, fosters creativity and innovation, and promotes individual and team growth. Empowered teams are more productive, engaged, and committed to the organization's goals and objectives. By setting clear goals and expectations, delegating authority and responsibility, providing resources and support, fostering a culture of collaboration, encouraging risk-taking and experimentation, and providing feedback and recognition, organizations

Sales rigor is an example of empowering teams. Here's my take on how important rigor is in the sales process and how you can leverage it to empower your teams.

The sales process is a critical component of any successful business, and rigor is a key ingredient in ensuring its success. Rigor refers to the level of structure, discipline, and accountability applied to the sales process, and it is essential to achieve consistent, repeatable results. In this blog post, we will explore the importance of rigor in the sales process and its impact on your sales team's performance.

1. **Increases accountability:** By implementing a rigorous sales process, you create a culture of accountability within your team. Everyone knows what is expected of them and the steps they need to take to achieve their goals. This structure helps to ensure everyone stays focused and committed to the process.

2. **Improves efficiency:** A rigorous sales process allows your team to work more efficiently by streamlining the steps they need to take to close a sale. This saves time and reduces the risk of missed opportunities.

3. **Facilitates continuous improvement:** Rigor in the sales process provides a framework for continuous improvement. By tracking and analyzing performance metrics, you can identify areas for improvement and adjust the process. Over time, this will result in a more effective and efficient sales process.

4. **Increases consistency:** Consistency is key to success in sales. By implementing a rigorous sales process, you ensure every sale is approached similarly, reducing the risk of outcome variability. This allows your team to focus on delivering consistent results.

5. **Supports collaboration:** A rigorous sales process can promote collaboration within your team. Everyone understands their role and the steps they need to take to achieve their goals, making it easier for team members to work together and support each other.

Rigor in the sales process is critical to achieving consistent, repeatable results. By increasing accountability, improving efficiency, facilitating continuous improvement, increasing consistency, and supporting collaboration, a rigorous sales process can help your team achieve its goals and drive success for your business.

Incorporating rigor into your sales process may take time and effort, but the benefits are clear. By focusing on structure, discipline, and accountability, you can create a sales process that delivers results and drives success for your team and your business. You're winning as a leader because you use rigor in the sales process to empower your teams.

Conversely, sales rigor can be used to micromanage.

Micromanagement is a management style where a manager or leader closely monitors and controls the work of their subordinates.

This approach can be detrimental to the morale of the team members and can lead to a demotivating work environment. This article will discuss the negative impact of micromanagement on corporate leadership roles and how it can lead to demotivation.

What is micromanagement?

Micromanagement is a management style where a manager or leader closely supervises and controls the work of their subordinates. This management style is characterized by a lack of trust and confidence in the team members and a need for constant control and involvement in all aspects of their work. Micromanagers often focus on the small details of a project rather than the bigger picture and can create a work environment that is demotivating and demoralizing.

The negative impact of micromanagement

Micromanagement can hurt both the team members and the manager or leader. Here are some of the most significant negative impacts of micromanagement:

Demotivation: Micromanagement can lead to a demotivating work environment. When team members feel like their manager doesn't trust or value their contributions, they can become demotivated and disengaged from their work.

Lack of creativity: Micromanagers can stifle creativity and innovation. Team members should be free to make decisions and take risks to avoid becoming complacent and unwilling to try new things.

Decreased productivity: Micromanagement can lead to decreased productivity. When team members are constantly being monitored and scrutinized, they may become anxious and hesitant to take action. This can lead to delays in completing tasks and projects.

Decreased job satisfaction: Micromanagement can lead to decreased job satisfaction. When team members feel like they have no control over their work and are constantly criticized, they may become unhappy in their jobs and start looking for other opportunities.

High turnover: Micromanagement can lead to high turnover rates. When team members feel like they are not valued or trusted, they may leave the organization searching for a better work environment.

How to avoid micromanagement in sales leadership roles

To avoid micromanagement in sales leadership roles, leaders must adopt a more collaborative and trusting approach to management. Here are strategies that can help:

Set clear expectations: Leaders need to set clear expectations for their team members. This includes defining goals, providing guidelines, and establishing timelines. When team members understand what is expected, they can work more independently and confidently.

Delegate responsibilities: Leaders need to delegate responsibilities to their team members. This involves assigning tasks and projects that align with their strengths and capabilities. Delegating responsibilities shows trust and confidence in the team members and allows them to take ownership of their work.

Provide resources and support: Leaders need to provide resources and support to their team members. This includes access to training and development opportunities and the tools and equipment to do their job effectively. Providing resources and support shows that the leader is invested in the success of their team members.

Foster open communication: Leaders must foster open communication with their team members. This involves listening to their ideas, concerns, and feedback and addressing them in a timely and respectful manner. Open communication builds trust and respect between the leader and the team members.

Provide feedback and recognition: Leaders need to provide feedback and recognition to their team members. This involves acknowledging their achievements, providing constructive feedback, and offering guidance and support when needed. Feedback and recognition motivate team members and show that their contributions are valued.

Micromanagement can hurt corporate leadership roles. It can lead to demotivation, decreased productivity, decreased job satisfaction, and high turnover rates. To avoid micromanagement, leaders need to adopt a more collaborative and trusting approach to management. This involves setting clear expectations, delegating responsibilities, providing resources and support, fostering open communication, and providing feedback and recognition.

Leaders should also be aware of their own management style and be willing to make changes when necessary. This includes being open to feedback from team members and recognizing when micromanagement tendencies are hindering the team's success.

When being productive, feeling micromanaged can have a significant impact on your ability to do things. Micromanagement is a management style where a manager closely observes or controls the work of their employees, often to an excessive degree. While micromanagement may be well-intentioned, it can negatively affect employees and their productivity.

One of the primary effects of micromanagement is that it can create a lack of trust between the manager and the employee. When an employee feels like their manager doesn't trust them to do their job, they may become anxious and second-guess themselves. This can lead to a decrease in productivity as the employee spends more time worrying about what their manager thinks of them than actually doing their work.

Micromanagement can also lead to a loss of motivation. Employees who feel like their manager is always looking over their shoulder may feel like their work isn't valued or appreciated. This can lead to disillusionment and a lack of motivation to do their best work. When employees are not motivated, they are less likely to complete tasks and may require constant reminders and follow-up from their manager.

Another impact of micromanagement is that it can stifle creativity and innovation. When employees feel they must follow specific rules and processes to the letter, they may be less likely to think outside the box or try new approaches to solve problems. This can lead to a lack of innovation within the company, which can be detrimental in today's rapidly changing business environment.

Micromanagement can also lead to increased stress levels for employees. Constantly feeling like they are under a microscope and being scrutinized can create a high-pressure work environment that is not conducive to productivity. When stressed, employees may have difficulty focusing on their work and become more prone to making mistakes, leading to even more scrutiny from their manager.

To combat the negative impact of micromanagement, there are several things that employees can do. First, it's essential to communicate with your manager. Let them know how you feel and provide examples of specific instances where their micromanagement has hurt your productivity. Approach the conversation professionally and constructively, with suggestions for working together to improve the situation.

It's also crucial to set clear expectations and boundaries with your manager. Let them know what you need to do your job effectively and efficiently, whether it's a specific amount of autonomy or regular check-ins to ensure that you are on the right track. Setting clear expectations can help your manager understand your needs and work together to create a productive and effective working relationship.

Another way to combat micromanagement is to focus on your own productivity. While it may be tempting to worry about what your manager thinks of you, it's essential to prioritize your own work and goals. By setting specific goals and working towards them, you can demonstrate your value to the company and build your confidence in your abilities.

Micromanaging can significantly impact productivity, motivation, creativity, and stress levels. By communicating with your manager, setting clear expectations and boundaries, and focusing on your own productivity, you can combat the negative impact of micromanagement and create a more productive and effective working relationship.

Micromanagement can have a significant negative impact on corporate leadership roles. It is important for leaders to adopt a more collaborative and trusting approach to management to avoid demotivation and ensure the success of the team. Leaders can create a positive work environment that motivates and engages team members by setting clear expectations, delegating responsibilities, providing resources and support, fostering open communication, and providing feedback and recognition.

In the Forbes article "10 Ways to Support and Motivate Remote Workers" by Haroon Ahmad says, "Recognize and celebrate employee successes. Recognizing your employees' accomplishments is crucial for building a positive remote work culture. This can include acknowledging individual or team achievements, sending congratulatory messages or cards, or hosting virtual celebrations. Recognizing and celebrating successes can help boost morale, foster a sense of community, and show employees that their hard work and contributions are valued."

The outcome of implementing these strategies is an empowered team.

Win-win.

Worksheet: Avoiding Micromanagement in Corporate Leadership Roles

Read each scenario below and answer the questions that follow. Think about how you would approach each situation to avoid micromanagement and create a more collaborative and trusting work environment.

Scenario 1:

You are the manager of a team of designers, and a new project requires a quick turnaround. You have a specific vision for the project and want to ensure it is executed exactly as you envision it.

What steps can you take to avoid micromanaging your team in this situation?

How can you communicate your vision and expectations to the team without micromanaging them?

How can you support the team to ensure they have the resources and tools they need to complete the project successfully?

Scenario 2:

You are a sales team leader, and you notice that one of your team members is struggling to meet its targets. You want to help them improve their performance, but you are concerned that providing too much feedback and oversight will come across as micromanaging.

How can you provide feedback to the team member without micromanaging them?

What strategies can you use to help the team member improve their performance without micromanaging them?

How can you build trust with the team member and show you are invested in their success without micromanaging them?

Scenario 3:

You are the director of a marketing department, and you have a team of experienced professionals used to working independently.

However, you recently took over the role and are still learning about the team's strengths and weaknesses.

How can you avoid micromanaging the team while ensuring they meet their objectives?

What strategies can you use to get to know the team members and their strengths and weaknesses without micromanaging them?

How can you delegate responsibilities to the team members while maintaining oversight and ensuring that the work is done effectively?

Scenario 4:

You are the manager of a customer service team, and you have noticed that one of your team members is frequently making mistakes impacting customer satisfaction.

How can you provide guidance and support to the team member without micromanaging them?

What strategies can you use to help the team member improve their performance without micromanaging them?

How can you build trust with the team member and show you are invested in their success without micromanaging them?

Reflection:

What strategies have you used in the past to avoid micromanaging your team members?

What strategies have most effectively created a collaborative and trusting work environment?

What strategies could you implement to avoid micromanaging your team members and create a more collaborative and trusting work environment?

Worksheet: Assessment of Current Team

Here's an assessment that Rachel can use to understand where her sales team is now and identify the best areas for starting to improve:

Current Sales Performance: What are the current sales performance metrics, such as revenue growth, win rates, deal velocity, and average deal size? How do these metrics compare to industry benchmarks and the company's historical performance?

Sales Process: How well-defined and effective is the sales process? Is there a clear sales methodology that the team follows? What are the key steps in the sales process, and what are the conversion rates at each stage?

Sales Pipeline: What is the size and quality of the sales pipeline? Are there enough opportunities to achieve the revenue targets? What is the average time to close a deal, and what is the conversion rate from pipeline to closed deals?

Sales Team: What is the current size and structure of the sales team? How well-equipped and trained are the sales reps? What are the key strengths and weaknesses of the team, and what are the opportunities for improvement?

Sales Tools and Technology: What sales tools and technology are in use? Are they effectively supporting the sales process? What are the key gaps and opportunities for improvement?

Sales Enablement: How well is the sales team enabled with the resources and support needed to sell effectively? Are there adequate marketing materials, product information, training, and other resources available to the team?

Sales Forecasting: How well is the sales team forecasting future sales performance? Is there a formal forecasting process in place? What is the accuracy of the forecasts, and what are the key drivers of forecast accuracy?

Customer Feedback: What is the feedback from customers about the sales experience? What are the key areas for improvement, and what are the sales team's strengths?

Competitive Landscape: What is the competitive landscape in the industry? Who are the key competitors, and what are their strengths and weaknesses? How is the sales team positioned relative to the competition, and what are the opportunities for differentiation?

By assessing these areas, Rachel can gain a comprehensive understanding of the current state of the sales team and identify the best areas to focus on for improvement.

Based on the assessment, Rachel can develop a targeted improvement plan that addresses the sales team's specific challenges and opportunities.

Chapter 11
Culture

Creating a Micro Culture Within Your Team

CART.

Collaboration. Accountability. Responsiveness. Transparency.

It was February 2021, and I was chatting with my team while attending an Executive all-hands in New Orleans. The idea was to come up with a culture code for our team. Something that weaves into the "accountability" fabric of our greater organization but is meaningful to us as a sales team.

What happened next was nothing short of amazing.

They started IM'ing back and forth a bunch of adjectives they felt we already embodied or should. They went on and on for several hours.

What we ended up with were "buckets" of adjectives similar to each other. For example, responsive, quick, and speedy all ended up in one bucket.

And at the end, we settled on four adjectives.

Then, Cynthia said, "Hey! If we put them in this order, they spell CART". And ever since, CART has been our team's culture. We reference the words daily in our interactions. We use the shopping cart icon on LinkedIn and completely dork out.

As Daniel Coyle says in *The Culture Code: The Secrets of Highly Successful Groups*, "One misconception about highly successful cultures is that they are happy, lighthearted places. This is mostly not the case. They are energized and engaged, but at their core, their members are oriented less around achieving happiness than around solving hard problems together. This task involves many moments of high-candor feedback and uncomfortable truth-telling when they confront the gap between where the group is and where it ought to be."

Establishing a positive culture within your sales team can greatly impact your business's success. When a company has a strong culture, it leads to happier, more motivated employees, which can increase productivity and result in better customer service.

I interviewed Brian Bosche, Co-Founder and CEO of the Purpose Company, and he had great things to say about teams, gratitude, and fulfillment.

There's this dynamic between purpose and fulfillment. Everybody is seeking some level of fulfillment in their life. Some people are seeking surface level happiness. Some people are seeking something much deeper than that. Purpose is the best of what you have to help others. Fulfillment on the other hand, is the result of helping others with the best of what you have. And human beings receive fulfillment in really three primary ways. One, gratitude from those we help two observation of the people we help. So for example, if you are an associate at a big four accounting firm, it's really important for your leader to let you know how you help the client so that that person can actually observe the transformation that the client had. The other way that we receive fulfillment is through our own personal results. So that could be the simple stuff. It could be getting a new car or getting a raise or something like that. But what most drives people is the gratitude they receive. And the biggest mistake that leaders make is they fail to give the people that report to them that are on their team specific gratitude, not general gratitude. Like, Hey John, thank you so much for being here today. Super glad you walked in the door. It's more like, Hey John, thank you so much for that spreadsheet tool you put together because that thing that we gave to the client today made literally the difference that closed the deal. I gotta thank you for that. If you didn't do that, that deal wouldn't have happened. That's an example of specific gratitude even better, is if you know that one of your team members has an incredibly high value skillset, make sure that you're connecting the gratitude, that specific dose of gratitude to the high value skillset. That's how you're going to tap into what most fulfills them. So remember purpose. If it's the best of what somebody has to help others, we have to make sure that we're highlighting the best of who they are in our gratitude, because that is completing a feedback loop of fulfillment. A lot of companies make a big mistake. Companies confuse compensation with gratitude. Compensation is not gratitude, compensation is contractual. Even bonuses really don't make a big difference. If you give somebody a raise, they've done studies on this, if you give somebody a raise, the average mental high that that gives somebody is about six weeks. So what are you going to do beyond compensation? It's not gratitude. You actually have to take the time to be grateful. You know, this is a person who's given their precious time, time, they're never going to get back to serve the mission of your company. We have to do better than compensation.

Here are tips for building a positive culture within your sales team:

One of the first steps in establishing a positive culture is to define your company's values. These values should be the foundation for all your actions and decisions as a team and should be communicated clearly to everyone. For example, if honesty and transparency are important values for your company, make sure that your sales team knows that they are expected to be honest with customers and with each other.

As a leader, it's important to lead by example. If you want your sales team to be positive, motivated, and hard-working, then you must model those behaviors yourself. Show your team that you are committed to the values that you have defined for your company.

Encouraging teamwork is another important aspect of building a positive culture within your sales team. While sales can be a competitive field, it's important to emphasize that everyone on the team is working towards the same goal. Encourage collaboration and celebrate successes as a team. This helps foster a sense of unity and support among team members.

In addition to teamwork, creating a culture of continuous learning and improvement is important. Sales is an ever-changing field, and it's important for your team to stay up to date on industry trends and best practices. Offer regular training opportunities and encourage team members to share their knowledge.

Recognition is also key to building a positive culture within your sales team. Acknowledge and celebrate successes, both big and small. This can include recognizing top performers, celebrating milestones, and showing appreciation for hard work. When team members feel valued and appreciated, they are more likely to be motivated and engaged.

Finally, it's important to create an open and supportive environment within your sales team. Encourage communication and collaboration, and make sure that team members feel comfortable sharing their ideas and concerns. When team members feel heard and supported, they are more likely to be engaged and committed to the team's goals.

Building a positive culture within your sales team is crucial for the success of your business. By defining your company's values, leading by example, encouraging teamwork and continuous learning, recognizing successes, and creating an open and supportive environment, you can help to create a strong and motivated team committed to achieving your business goals.

Worksheet: Creating a Culture in Your Sales Team

Once you have completed this worksheet, use it as a guide for creating a plan to build a strong culture in your sales team.

Remember to involve your team members, seek their feedback and input, and communicate your plan clearly and frequently.

Building a strong culture takes time and effort, but with commitment and perseverance, you can create a team that is motivated, engaged, and driven to succeed.

Define your core values:

1. List three to five core values you want to define your sales team's culture.
2. For each value, please briefly describe what it means to you and how it aligns with your company's mission and goals.
3. Communicate your expectations: List three to five expectations you have for your sales team in terms of behavior, performance, and results.
4. For each expectation, provide specific examples of what success looks like.
5. Foster a positive work environment. List three to five strategies you can use to create a positive work environment in your sales team.
6. Please explain how you plan to implement each strategy and what you hope to achieve.
7. Lead by example. List three to five behaviors and values you want to model as a leader.
8. For each behavior and value, explain why it is important and how you plan to demonstrate it.
9. Invest in training and development. List three to five areas of training and development you want to invest in for your sales team.
10. For each area, explain why it is essential and what resources you plan to use to provide training and support.
11. Recognize and reward outstanding performance:
12. List three to five ways you can recognize and reward outstanding performance in your sales team.

13. For each way, explain how it aligns with your core values and how you plan to implement it.
14. Measure and track progress. List three to five metrics you want to track to measure progress toward your sales team's goals.
15. For each metric, explain how you plan to track it and your actions based on the results.

Chapter 12
Leading With Empathy

"Always keep the customer at the core of everything you do: every touchpoint, every thought, every research, every presentation. And teaching your team to do the same. If you keep the customer at the core, I'm convinced that everything else will fall into place." – Allison McDougall, EVP Sales

Leading with empathy is a powerful leadership strategy that can help to create a positive and productive work environment. Empathy involves understanding and sharing the feelings and experiences of others and using that understanding to guide your interactions and decision-making as a leader. By leading with empathy, you can build strong relationships with your team members, promote open communication, and foster a sense of belonging and mutual respect.

Alissa Lieppman, Vice President and Head of Culture says, "One thing that I've learned a lot about leadership styles, what's important to the people that work around you and how to lead with that influence versus just a direct reporting structure."

One key aspect of leading with empathy is active listening. Active listening involves giving full attention to the person speaking and trying to understand their perspective. When you actively listen to your team members, you show you value their thoughts and feelings and that you will consider their ideas and feedback.

To practice active listening, give your team members your undivided attention when they speak to you. This means putting aside distractions like your phone or computer and making eye contact to show you are fully engaged. As they talk, ask questions and clarify any unclear points. Repeat what you've heard to confirm your understanding and avoid interrupting or jumping to conclusions.

Another way to lead with empathy is to show appreciation for your team members. Expressing gratitude can help to boost morale and foster a sense of camaraderie. Acknowledge your team members' contributions and achievements and let them know their hard work is valued.

To show appreciation, give a simple thank-you note or verbal praise. You could offer incentives like bonuses or extra time off for exceptional work. Whatever approach you choose, make sure that your appreciation is specific and personalized to each individual team member.

In addition to active listening and showing appreciation, another critical aspect of leading with empathy is demonstrating understanding and compassion. This means putting yourself in your team member's shoes and trying to understand their perspectives and experiences. When your team members feel you know and care about their needs and concerns, they are more likely to feel motivated and committed to their work.

To demonstrate understanding and compassion, start by trying to learn more about your team members' personal and professional goals. Take the time to understand their challenges and what motivates them, and work to provide the support and resources they need to succeed. When conflicts or issues arise, take a collaborative approach to resolve them and work together to find solutions beneficial for everyone involved.

Another important way to demonstrate understanding and compassion is to be flexible and accommodating when necessary. This might involve offering flexible work hours, providing extra support or resources for team members struggling, or being understanding when team members need to take time off for personal reasons. By being flexible and understanding, you can create a positive and supportive work environment that fosters loyalty and commitment among your team members.

Finally, leading with empathy involves promoting diversity, equity, and inclusion within your team. This means creating a work environment welcoming and supportive of people from all backgrounds and perspectives and ensuring everyone feels valued and included.

To promote diversity, equity, and inclusion, start by educating yourself and your team members about the importance of these values. Be aware of any biases or assumptions that might impact your interactions with others, and work to overcome them. Encourage open communication and collaboration, and ensure everyone's voice is heard and respected.

Another important way to promote diversity, equity, and inclusion is to create professional growth and development opportunities. This might involve offering mentorship or coaching programs or providing access to training and development resources to help your team members build their skills and advance their careers. By investing in your team members' professional growth and development, you can build a more diverse and inclusive team that is better equipped to meet future challenges.

In conclusion, leading with empathy is a powerful way to build strong relationships with your team members, promote open communication, and create a positive and productive work environment. By actively listening, showing appreciation, demonstrating understanding and compassion, and promoting diversity, equity, and inclusion, you can help to create a team that is motivated, engaged, and committed to achieving your organization's goals. While leading with empathy requires effort and intentionality, the benefits to your team and your organization are well worth it. By putting empathy at the center of your leadership style, you can build a team that is resilient, adaptable, and successful in the long term.

Chapter 13
Managing Up

Tell Them What They Want, Give Them What They Need

Managing up refers to the art of effectively influencing and working with one's superiors. It is a critical skill that enables employees to navigate the corporate landscape and achieve their professional goals while contributing to the organization's success. Managing up is especially essential regarding the executive team, as these individuals hold significant decision-making power and can significantly affect an employee's career trajectory.

Managing your executive team is a critical skill that can help you achieve your professional goals and contribute to the success of your organization. By building strong relationships, understanding their goals and priorities, anticipating their needs, communicating effectively, demonstrating your value, being proactive, and managing expectations, you can establish yourself as a valuable team player and earn the trust and respect of your executive team.

Managing up is a two-way street. Your executive team has a responsibility to support and guide you, provide feedback, and offer opportunities for growth and development. Be receptive to their feedback and suggestions and use them to improve your work and enhance your skills.

Here are strategies to "manage up" to your executive team effectively.

Understand their goals and priorities.

It's crucial to understand your executive team's goals and priorities to align your work and communication with what they want to achieve. Research and analyze the executive team's priorities, read their speeches and articles and ask questions to your direct supervisor or other relevant people for a better understanding. Once you understand well, you can tailor your communication to demonstrate how your work supports their goals and objectives.

Anticipate their needs

Anticipating the needs of your executive team is another critical aspect of managing up. Anticipate their needs and proactively offer solutions. When preparing reports or presentations, expect the types of questions that may arise and prepare answers in advance. By anticipating their needs, you will demonstrate your value as a proactive team player and reduce the need for your executive team to micromanage your work.

Communicate effectively

Communication is a key component of managing up. Be clear, concise, and respectful when communicating with your executive team. Avoid jargon or technical language that may be difficult for them to understand. Present information in a way that is easy to digest and use. When presenting ideas or recommendations, provide supporting data and explain how your proposal aligns with the executive team's goals and objectives. Finally, keep your communication open and transparent, and don't hesitate to ask questions or seek clarification when necessary.

Demonstrate your value

Demonstrating your value is essential to managing up successfully. Identify areas where you can add value to your executive team and the organization as a whole. Take on projects or responsibilities that align with your executive team's goals and objectives and demonstrate how your work contributes to the organization's success. Be proactive in identifying problems and offering solutions, and take ownership of your work to ensure it is completed to a high standard.

Be proactive

Being proactive is crucial when managing up. Stay informed about industry trends and developments and offer suggestions on how the organization can stay ahead of the curve. Identify opportunities for improvement and present your ideas to your executive team. By being proactive, you will demonstrate your commitment to the organization's success and show you are invested in the company's long-term growth.

Manage expectations

Managing expectations is critical when managing up. Be realistic about what you can deliver and set achievable goals for yourself. Be transparent about your workload and priorities, and communicate any potential roadblocks or challenges that may impact your ability to deliver on time. Managing expectations is crucial to building trust with your executive team and ensuring that you can deliver high-quality work consistently.

Build strong relationships

Building a strong relationship with your executive team is the foundation for managing up effectively. Take the time to get to know your executives as individuals, understand their priorities and challenges, and demonstrate a genuine interest in their success. Please try to connect with them on a personal level by engaging in conversations that go beyond work-related topics. Building a strong relationship will increase the likelihood of your executive team being receptive to your ideas and suggestions.

Worksheet: Evaluating Pseudo-Performance in a Managing Up Example

Below is a scenario. As you're reading through the goals and problems, the idea is to think of how Rachel can better manage up and help her develop a game plan to report the solution to her problem to achieve her goals to her C-level.

Name: Rachel Williams

Age: 43

Occupation: Chief Revenue Officer (CRO)

Background: Rachel Williams is a highly accomplished executive with over 20 years of experience in the tech industry. She has a proven track record of driving revenue growth and profitability for large and small companies. Rachel was recently appointed as the CRO of a fast-growing software development and IT services company. Her main focus is to drive revenue growth and optimize the company's revenue streams.

Goals and Challenges:

Rachel's primary goal as the CRO is to drive revenue growth and profitability for the company. She will be responsible for developing and implementing revenue strategies, identifying new revenue streams, and optimizing existing ones. Rachel's biggest challenge will be to ensure that the company can scale its revenue while maintaining quality and profitability. She must work closely with other departments, such as sales, marketing, and product development, to ensure everyone is aligned and working towards the same goals.

Another challenge that Rachel will face is navigating a rapidly changing market, which includes emerging technologies, new competitors, and changing customer needs. She will need to stay current with the latest trends and technologies in the industry and be prepared to adapt the company's revenue strategies accordingly.

Personality:

Rachel is a dynamic and results-driven executive passionate about driving revenue growth and profitability. She is a strategic thinker able to see the big picture and identify opportunities for growth and improvement. Rachel is also a skilled communicator able to articulate her vision and goals to her team and stakeholders.

Rachel is a collaborative leader who understands the importance of working closely with other departments and stakeholders to achieve the company's revenue goals. She is a problem solver able to identify and address revenue challenges quickly and effectively. Overall, Rachel is a confident and experienced CRO committed to driving revenue growth and profitability for her company.

PROBLEM

As a CRO, Rachel will face various challenges and problems to address to achieve her revenue goals. Here are examples:

Ensuring Revenue Growth: One of the main challenges that Rachel will face as a CRO is ensuring consistent revenue growth for the company. She will need to develop and implement revenue strategies that are both scalable and sustainable and that consider changing market dynamics, customer needs, and emerging technologies.

Managing Revenue Streams: Another challenge that Rachel will face is managing the revenue streams of the company, including products, services, and partnerships. She will need to optimize existing revenue streams to ensure they are profitable and align with the company's overall revenue goals. She will also need to identify new revenue streams and partnerships to help the company diversify its revenue and reduce risk.

Aligning Sales and Marketing: A common problem many companies face is more alignment between the sales and marketing departments. As the CRO, Rachel must ensure that these departments work together effectively to drive revenue growth. She will need to develop a shared understanding of the company's revenue goals and the target customer and ensure that the sales and marketing teams have the resources and tools to succeed.

Managing Data and Analytics: Another challenge that Rachel will face is managing the data and analytics needed to make informed revenue decisions. She will need to ensure that the company has access to accurate and timely data and that the data is being used effectively to drive revenue growth. Rachel will also need to ensure that the company has the necessary analytics tools and expertise to analyze and interpret the data.

Managing People: As the CRO, Rachel will be responsible for managing a team of revenue professionals, including sales, marketing, and partnerships. She must ensure the team has the skills, training, and resources to achieve the company's revenue goals. Rachel must also motivate and inspire her team and create a culture of excellence and continuous improvement.

Pricing Strategy: Pricing can be complex and difficult to navigate, particularly for companies that offer a range of products or services. Rachel will need to develop and implement a pricing strategy that is both competitive and profitable while also ensuring that the company's products and services are perceived as valuable by customers. This may require market research, competitor analysis, and collaboration with other departments, such as product development and finance.

Talent Acquisition and Retention: As the company grows and evolves, Rachel will need to ensure that the company has the right talent to achieve its revenue goals. This may require developing a talent acquisition strategy, identifying key roles and skill sets, and creating a culture that attracts and retains top talent. Rachel will also need to work with other departments to ensure that the company provides opportunities for career growth and development for its employees.

Managing Risk: As the CRO, Rachel will need to ensure that the company is managing risk effectively to achieve its revenue goals. This may involve identifying and mitigating risks related to market changes, regulatory issues, cybersecurity, or other factors that could affect the company's revenue streams. Rachel will need to work with other departments, such as legal and finance, to ensure that the company is following best practices and complies with relevant regulations and policies.

Chapter 14
Key Performance Indicators

Under Promise Over Deliver

As a Sales leader, there are several KPIs (Key Performance Indicators) that are important to the board when managing up to the executive team. These KPIs are used to measure the effectiveness of the Sales team and the impact of the Sales department on the overall performance of the organization. Some of the key KPIs that are important to the board include:

Sales Revenue: Sales revenue is the total amount of revenue generated by the Sales department over a specific period. This KPI is crucial to the board because it directly affects the financial performance of the organization.

Sales Growth: Sales growth measures the percentage increase in sales revenue over a specific period. This KPI is important because it shows whether the Sales department is growing and expanding its customer base.

Customer Acquisition Cost (CAC): CAC measures the cost of acquiring a new customer. This KPI is important to the board because it shows how much the organization spends to acquire new customers and whether these costs are sustainable.

Customer Lifetime Value (CLTV): CLTV measures the total value a customer brings to the organization over their lifetime. This KPI is important to the board because it shows the long-term impact of the Sales department on the organization's financial performance.

Sales Conversion Rate: Sales conversion rate measures the percentage of leads converted into customers. This KPI is important to the board because it shows the effectiveness of the Sales department in converting leads into customers.

Sales Pipeline: Sales pipeline measures the total value of all the opportunities in the Sales pipeline. This KPI is important to the board because it shows the potential revenue that the Sales department can generate.

Sales Cycle Length: Sales cycle length measures the time to close a deal from the initial contact to the final sale. This KPI is important to the board because it shows the effectiveness of the Sales department in closing deals and generating revenue.

Customer Satisfaction (CSAT): CSAT measures customers' satisfaction with the organization's products and services. This KPI is important to the board because it shows the Sales department's ability to provide high-quality products and services that meet customer needs.

When managing up to the executive team as a Sales leader, it is important to focus on KPIs that directly affect the organization's financial performance, such as sales revenue, sales growth, CAC, and CLTV. It is also important to focus on KPIs that measure the effectiveness of the Sales department in converting leads into customers and providing high-quality products and services that meet customer needs, such as sales conversion rate, sales cycle length, and CSAT. By focusing on these KPIs, Sales leaders can demonstrate the impact of the Sales department on the organization's performance and earn the trust and support of the executive team.

Worksheet: Tracking and Reporting on KPIs

Objective: To identify and track key performance indicators (KPIs) that are important to the board when managing up to the executive team as a Sales leader. Managing up to your executive team as a Sales leader requires a focus on key performance indicators that are important to the board. By tracking these KPIs, setting targets, and regularly reviewing the data, Sales leaders can demonstrate the impact of the Sales department on the organization's financial performance and customer satisfaction. The worksheet template provided can serve as a guide for Sales leaders to create their own KPI tracking system and effectively manage up to their executive team.

Instructions: Identify the KPIs that are important to the board when managing up to the executive team as a Sales leader. Refer to the list of KPIs provided in this chapter.

1. Determine the frequency of measurement for each KPI (e.g., weekly, monthly, quarterly, etc.)
2. Set targets for each KPI based on your organization's goals and past performance.
3. Create a table or spreadsheet to track each KPI, its target, and actual performance.
4. Set up a system for collecting and analyzing data for each KPI (e.g., CRM system, sales reports, customer surveys, etc.)
5. Review the data regularly and make adjustments as necessary to ensure that you are on track to meet your targets.
6. Use the data to identify areas of strength and weakness in the Sales department and develop action plans to address any issues.
7. Communicate the KPI data and progress to the executive team in a clear and concise manner, highlighting achievements and opportunities for improvement.
8. Use the KPI data to demonstrate the impact of the Sales department on the organization's financial performance and customer satisfaction.

Worksheet: Measuring your sales team against the pipeline

Here's an assessment that Rachel can use to measure the people in her team against their pipeline:

Pipeline Size: What is the size of each salesperson's pipeline, and how does it compare to their peers? Is the pipeline sufficient to achieve revenue targets, and are there any gaps or areas of concern?

Pipeline Quality: How qualified are the opportunities in each salesperson's pipeline? What is the level of engagement and interest from the prospects, and how likely are they to close? Are there any weak spots or bottlenecks in the pipeline?

Pipeline Velocity: What is the velocity of the pipeline, and how does it compare to industry benchmarks and historical performance? What is the average time to close deals, and are there any outliers or areas of concern?

Pipeline Conversion: What is the conversion rate of each salesperson's pipeline, and how does it compare to their peers and industry benchmarks? What are the key drivers of pipeline conversion, and what are the opportunities for improvement?

Salesperson Performance: How well is each salesperson performing against their pipeline? Are they meeting their revenue targets, and what are their win rate and deal velocity? How does their performance compare to their peers and historical performance?

Salesperson Capability: What is the capability and skill level of each salesperson? How well-equipped are they to manage their pipeline effectively? What are their key strengths and weaknesses, and what are the opportunities for improvement?

Sales Coaching: How effective are the coaching and support provided to each salesperson? Are they receiving the feedback, guidance, and resources needed to improve their pipeline performance? What are the opportunities for improvement in coaching and support?

Sales Culture: What is the culture and mindset within the sales team? Is there a focus on pipeline management and improvement, or are there other priorities taking precedence? What are the opportunities for building a more pipeline-focused culture?

By assessing these areas, Rachel can gain a comprehensive understanding of how well each salesperson is managing their pipeline and identify the best opportunities for improvement. Based on the assessment, Rachel can develop targeted coaching and development plans that address the specific challenges and opportunities facing each salesperson. This can drive overall pipeline performance and improve the sales team's ability to achieve their revenue targets.

Chapter 15
Personal & Professional Growth Plan

Passion Project

As the saying goes, leaders are not born; they are made. Leadership growth is all about recognizing that leadership skills can be developed and honed over time through learning, practice, and experience.

Whether you are an aspiring leader or an established one, it is essential to understand that leadership growth is a continuous process. It requires a commitment to self-improvement and a willingness to learn from feedback and mistakes. In this blog post, we will explore key ideas and strategies for achieving leadership growth.

The article "Cascading Goals: Aligning Your Team's Goals with Your Business Objectives" by Arootah says, "Effective goal cascading requires clear communication and alignment across all levels of the organization. Leaders must clearly communicate the company's mission, vision, and objectives, and ensure that everyone understands how their individual goals contribute to the larger goals of the organization. This requires ongoing communication and feedback, as well as a commitment to transparency and accountability."

Embrace a Growth Mindset

Leadership growth starts with the right mindset. A growth mindset is a belief that one's abilities and qualities can be developed through effort and dedication. Embracing a growth mindset means being open to new challenges, seeking feedback, and being willing to learn from mistakes.

Focus on Developing Core Leadership Skills

Certain core leadership skills essential for success include communication, collaboration, strategic thinking, and decision-making. To achieve leadership growth, it is essential to focus on developing these skills through training, coaching, and practice.

Build Relationships and Networks

Leadership is not just about individual skills but also about building relationships and networks. To be an effective leader, you need to build trust and rapport with your team, peers, and stakeholders. This requires active listening, empathy, and the ability to communicate effectively.

Seek Out Mentors and Role Models

One of the most effective ways to achieve leadership growth is to seek mentors and role models. Mentors can provide guidance, support, and advice based on their experiences. Role models can inspire and motivate you to develop your leadership style and approach.

Alissa Lippman, Vice President and Head of Culture, suggests what works for her. "I watched and I observed. I looked at the leaders that I wanted to embody. I took different approaches from my current managers that I would say, here's what I want to do, just like you, here's what I want to do a little bit differently. And started to develop my own leadership style that I felt that I could connect with the team members that I worked with."

Take Risks and Learn from Failure

Leadership growth requires taking risks and being willing to learn from failure. This means stepping outside your comfort zone, trying new things, and being open to feedback. Failure is an inevitable part of the learning process, and successful leaders know how to use failure as a learning opportunity.

Leadership growth is a continuous process that requires a growth mindset, a focus on developing core skills, building relationships and networks, seeking mentors and role models, and taking risks and learning from failure. Adopting these strategies allows you to develop your leadership abilities and succeed in your career.

Adding to your skillset professionally should be a lifelong process.

If you have 20 or 40 years of experience in your role, it's understandable to feel confident in your abilities. However, even experienced leaders can benefit from reading management books.

Here are a few reasons:

Refresh your perspective: Even if you have been managing for a long time, staying open to new ideas and perspectives is important. Reading management books can help you refresh your perspective on management and provide you with new ideas and strategies to try.

Learn about emerging trends: The business world is constantly evolving, and new trends and best practices in management are always emerging. Reading management books can help you stay current with the latest trends and techniques, which can help you be a more effective manager.

Develop new skills: Even if you are experienced in management, there may be areas where you can improve your skills. A management book can help you identify areas where you can improve and guide you through how to develop new skills.

Refine your approach: No manager is perfect, and there is always room for improvement. Reading management books helps you identify areas where you can refine your approach and become an even better manager.

Learn from others' experiences: Even experienced managers can benefit from learning from the experiences of others. A management book can provide insights into how other successful managers have approached common management challenges.

In summary, while you may have a lot of experience managing salespeople, reading management books can help you refresh your perspective, learn about emerging trends, develop new skills, refine your approach, and learn from others' experiences. By staying open to new ideas and continuing to learn, you can become an even more effective manager.

Chapter 16
Lead Beyond Your Role

Always Be Innovating

In 2022 I helped my direct report, Belinda, successfully propose and execute her first localization industry panel at the LocWorld conference with other industry leaders, Edith Bendermacher, Ana Trejo, and Katell Jentreau, titled How Globalization ROI Intersects with Customer Experience in a Fast-changing World.

Not only did she personally do well, but the room was packed, and the feedback was overwhelmingly positive.

But this didn't come easy.

We started in January 2022 with the idea that she would host a panel discussion at an industry conference. She had seen me do it in the years prior. Not only was it an honor to be recognized as a panel host, but it was also extremely educational and insightful.

I always say you can lead a horse to water, but you can't make them drink.

So it wasn't enough I wanted this for her.

She had to want it for herself and take actionable purpose-driven steps toward achieving this goal.

What started as tracking it as a yearly goal remained stagnant most of the year.

She wasn't sure where to start when the conference announced its call for papers.

I contacted Edith, whom I used to work with at NetApp, and asked if she was interested in collaborating. She said of course!

From there, the path was laid for Belinda to meet with Edith, strategize on the topic content and pull in two other speakers who would round out the panel with different perspectives.

But then the work began!

To add her value, Belinda took notes of all pre-conference meetings, coordinated multiple rounds of edits for the submission, organized prep calls, and moderated the panel.

Phew.

Contributing to an industry event is one way you can lead beyond your role. Another way is to take on extra assignments at your company – like the year I volunteered to own CSAT. And my favorite is to drive innovation.

Did I tell you about my Outcomes Based Framework, which won a Bronze Stevie Award in March 2023?

Here are three hacks to help you get out of your own way and grow beyond your leadership role:

Practice self-awareness: It's important to be aware of limiting beliefs and self-doubt. One way to do this is through journaling or regular reflection time. Write down negative thoughts or beliefs holding you back and challenge them with evidence to the contrary. This can help you shift your mindset and get out of your own way.

Seek feedback: Ask for feedback from your team, colleagues, and mentors. This can be uncomfortable, but it's important to hear positive and negative feedback to improve. Listen carefully to what others say and take it as an opportunity for growth and learning.

Embrace failure: Failure is a natural part of the learning process, and it's important to embrace it as an opportunity for growth. Rather than viewing failure as a reflection of your abilities, see it as a chance to learn and improve. Take full accountability for your actions and learn from your mistakes to improve next time.

Overall, getting out of your own way and growing beyond your leadership role requires self-awareness, feedback, and a willingness to embrace failure. By practicing these three hacks, you can take full accountability for your new role and become a more effective leader.

Worksheet: Identifying a passion project within your role

Here's a worksheet that can help someone identify a passion project that aligns with their personal and professional growth goals as a sales leader:

Step 1: Identify Personal and Professional Growth Goals

Reflect on your personal and professional goals as a sales leader. Consider what skills, knowledge, or experience you would like to develop, as well as what areas of personal growth you would like to focus on.

Write down your top three goals in the space below.

1

2

3

Step 2: Brainstorm Potential Passion Projects

Think about projects or initiatives that could help you achieve your personal and professional growth goals. These could be related to your current role, or they could be outside of your immediate responsibilities.

Brainstorm a list of potential passion projects in the space below.

1

2

3

Step 3: Evaluate Passion Projects

Review your list of potential passion projects and evaluate each based on these criteria:

- Alignment with personal and professional growth goals
- Feasibility and resources required
- Potential impact on your team or organization

Rank each passion project on a scale of 1-5 (1 being low and 5 being high) for each criterion.

Potential Passion Project 1: _____

Criteria	Score
Alignment with goals	
Feasibility/resources	
Impact on team/org	

Potential Passion Project 2: _____

Criteria	Score
Alignment with goals	
Feasibility/resources	
Impact on team/org	

Potential Passion Project 3: _____

Criteria	Score
Alignment with goals	
Feasibility/resources	
Impact on team/org	

Step 4: Select a Passion Project

Select the passion project with the highest total score based on your evaluation. This project should align most closely with your personal and professional growth goals, is feasible given the resources available, and has the potential to significantly impact your team or organization.

Selected Passion Project:

Step 5: Create a Plan

Develop a plan for how you will pursue your passion project. This should include:

- Specific goals and objectives for the project
- A timeline for completion
- Required resources (e.g., budget, team members)
- Action steps and milestones
- Metrics for measuring success

Write your plan below and refer to it regularly to track your progress and stay focused on your passion project.

Passion Project Plan:

Goals/Objectives:

Timeline:

Resources:

Action Steps/Milestones:

Metrics for success:

Worksheet: Brainstorming Innovation with Cross-Functional Teams to Drive Sales Results

Use this worksheet to brainstorm **innovative ideas and solutions for improving sales performance in collaboration with cross-functional teams.**

Follow the steps below to guide your brainstorming session.

Step 1: Define the Problem

Identify the specific problem or challenge you are facing in terms of sales performance. Please write it down in the space below.

Problem:

Step 2: Identify Cross-Functional Teams

Identify the cross-functional teams that may have a stake in improving sales performance. Write them down in the space below.

Cross-Functional Teams:

Step 3: Brainstorm Innovative Solutions

With your cross-functional teams, brainstorm innovative solutions to the problem you identified in Step 1. Use the questions below to guide your discussion.

Questions to Consider:

1. What are some potential solutions to the problem we identified?
2. What are new ideas we could try we haven't tried before?

3. What are ways we could leverage technology to improve sales performance?
4. What are ways we could improve collaboration between cross-functional teams?
5. What are ways we could improve communication with customers?

Other questions:

Step 4: Prioritize Ideas

Review the ideas generated during the brainstorming session and prioritize them based on feasibility, impact, and alignment with business goals. Write down the top three ideas in the space below.

Top Three Ideas:

Step 5: Assign Roles and Responsibilities

Assign roles and responsibilities to each team member involved in implementing the action plan. Write down the roles and responsibilities for each idea in the space below.

Roles and Responsibilities:

Step 6: Set Timeline and Metrics

Set a timeline for each action plan and identify metrics for measuring success. Write down the timeline and metrics for each idea in the space below.

Timeline and Metrics:

Step 7: Assign Roles and Responsibilities

Assign roles and responsibilities to each team member to implement the action plan. Write down the roles and responsibilities for each idea in the space below.

Roles and Responsibilities::

Step 7: Set Timeline and Metrics

Set a timeline for each action plan and identify metrics for measuring success. Write down the timeline and metrics for each idea in the space below.

Timeline and Metrics::

Step 8: Develop an Action Plan

Develop an action plan outlining the steps needed to implement each of the top three ideas. Write down the action plan for each idea in the space below.

Action Plan:

Idea #1:

Step 1:

Step 2:

Step 3:

Step 4:

Step 5:

Step 6:

Step 7:

Step 8:

Timeline:

Metrics:

Idea #2:

Step 1:

Step 2:

Step 3:

Step 4:

Step 5:

Step 6:

Step 7:

Step 8:

Timeline:

Metrics:

Idea #3:

Step 1:

Step 2:

Step 3:

Step 4:

Step 5:

Step 6:

Step 7:

Step 8:

Timeline:

Metrics:

Step 9: Review and Refine

Review progress regularly and refine the action plan as needed to ensure success. Schedule regular meetings with cross-functional teams to discuss progress, identify roadblocks, and make necessary adjustments.

Conclusion:

Brainstorming innovative solutions with cross-functional teams is a powerful way for sales leaders to drive results and improve sales performance.

Chapter 17
Do The Damn Thing

LFG!!!!

One of my favorite things to say to my team and to myself is to "do the damn thing." And that's exactly what I would say here.

Becoming a better sales leader requires action and commitment to continuous growth. You must get uncomfortable, have an unpopular opinion, be the best version of yourself, fail forward, ask lots of questions, and rely on others.

Like Allison McDougall says, "Find your joy every single day."

The first pillar of unlocking greatness within your team is to get out of your own way.

Acknowledge and address any limiting beliefs, biases, or habits that may hinder your success. Focus on developing a growth mindset and embracing a culture of learning and experimentation. Find mentors and stay committed to the process. You can do it!

The second pillar is all about Implementing failing forward, analyzing your team's daily sales habits, empowering your teams, looking at culture, leading with empathy, and managing up and understanding KPIs.

The third and final pillar is to continue to grow personally and professionally. Attend conferences, read books and articles, seek mentorship, and invest in ongoing training and development opportunities. Stay up to date with industry trends and best practices and remain curious and open-minded.

By taking these steps, you can elevate your leadership and sales skills, build stronger relationships with your team and customers, and achieve more tremendous success and fulfillment in your career. So don't wait - start acting today to be a better sales leader!

I love to help companies develop and implement sales strategies through workshops and training - not only theory but actionable takeaways to implement right away.

For example, I love to help clients get immediate transformational results in a workshop designed to help your capable teams combat burnout, stay engaged, find self-fulfillment, boost creativity, drive innovation, and improve social selling.

I would love to hear your thoughts next time you try these strategies. And I cannot wait to see how you evolve as a leader! Please tag us #beabettersalesleader on social media.

If you're looking for help, please reach out:

hello@beabettersalesleader.com

Made in the USA
Las Vegas, NV
08 May 2024

89701205R00066